CW00853897

Sorry, It's Not My Department

Where the money really goes in your town hall and the ways public services can be improved.

By

Rob Tape

DEDICATION

This book (for what it is worth) is for my amazing wife. Without her patience and support I would not have been able to write a word. She makes it all worthwhile.

CONTENTS

ACKNOWLEDGMENTS

Thank you to all those people who I have been lucky enough to work with over the last few years. Despite my cynicism over the public sector; I have worked with some absolute stars – although not many, admittedly. Not enough to make everything alright but just enough to make me think that not all is lost.

So to all those people, thank you and you have taught me a lot.

"This is the true joy of life, the being used up for a purpose recognised by yourself as a mighty one; being a force of nature instead of a feverish little clot of ailments and grievances, complaining that the world will not devote itself to making you happy. I am of the opinion that my life belongs to the community, and as long as I live, it is my privilege to do for it what I can."

– George Bernard Shaw

Introduction

"My Dad works for the Council, and he's so fast he finishes work at 5 o' clock but is always home by 2 o'clock."

– Ken Dodd

The financial waste in the public sector is something that has been well documented in recent years. Many articles have thrown light on the bureaucratic waste in central government spending and headlines along the lines of 'Broken Britain' or 'Gone to the Dogs' certainly popularise the issues and tap into the national feeling of cynicism towards the public sector. However, many of these have had a hidden (or in some cases not so hidden) political agenda and have failed to address the main underlying problems. Instead they have been an opportunity for finger pointing, rumour mongering and much 'tut-tutting' from onlookers.

Lots of authors have spent time analysing and critiquing national government and the mistakes it has made in spending our tax money over the last decade on this IT system or that defence programme. Specific public services have been revealed warts and all by authors like Frank Chalk (Schools), Theodore Dalrymple (NHS), and Inspector Gadget and PC David Copperfield (Police). Local authorities have, for the most part, escaped pretty much unscathed from this commentary.

The quote above probably reflects the view that many people have of the average council. And, frankly, given the state of councils and the public sector in general, who can blame them? My intention is to try and explain how local town halls really operate and to show that things are neither quite as wonderful as some people would have you believe nor quite as bad as others would like you to think.

My background is straightforward enough and is similar to thousands of others out there: school, college, a job in the private sector working in sales followed by a 'conversion' to the public sector early in my career (I use the term loosely) where I have been working ever since. After twenty years in various councils across the country I have reached the dizzy heights of middle management. I have become that person most resented by the taxpayer. My position has neither glamour nor status but, believe it or not, my job is very rewarding despite all the problems outlined in this book, and this is the reason I still enjoy going to work.

This book is, I admit, a selfish excuse for me to unleash my frustrations at the idiocy, bureaucracy and sheer bad management that I see almost every day in the town hall. However, I also hope that it makes people more aware of some of the things that go on and inspires some thinking about how things need to change. Nothing more and nothing less. If the managers, coordinators and politicians want to take heed then I hope they will, but as you progress through the book you will see why I won't be holding my breath for this to happen.

I do not claim to be completely apolitical; few people can genuinely say that, but in this book I have tried to remove the party politics from my arguments. The examples given are used as demonstrations and are not intended to point the finger of blame at the incumbent politicians. The public sector is such a complex and interlinked structure that to try and solve things with the sweeping statement of, "Labour did this" or, "The Conservatives did that," is an over-simplification.

My view is a straight forward one; whether councils want to spend billions on the delivery of public services or to cut back and spend as little as possible, the overriding principle should be the same. Every pound should be spent efficiently and effectively. Waste, bureaucracy, and duplication should be eradicated wherever possible. Whether the savings are returned to the public coffers or reinvested to make front line services more productive is a political decision and one for the elected representatives of the day.

I have tried to avoid laying too much blame with people (although there is plenty to go round) and, instead, take a more practical look at the public sector by giving examples of waste, touching briefly on some of the possible solutions and hopefully asking the powers that be why they are not doing more.

All I ask you to remember from each chapter and each example is that every single pound wasted means one pound not spent on actually delivering services. The examples I give might be mirrored in private businesses but as far as I'm concerned they can do what they want; if they want to spend customers' money on daft ideas and vast bureaucracies that's up to them. As a customer you can always get your baked beans, mobile phone or car from somewhere else if you wish. Local public sector organisations, however, have more responsibility and must manage *your* money with greater care.

I genuinely hope you enjoy the book and find it interesting. It is purely my opinion; it is not a party political broadcast and it's not trying to change the world. But hopefully it will get everyone thinking and questioning just a little bit more.

2. What Do I Pay My (Council) Taxes For Anyway?

While it may not be a widely held view, your local council has more impact on the average UK citizen than almost any public sector organisation in the UK. While our national security and defence departments do an important job protecting the country they are not services that most people see anything of on a practical level throughout their lives. The police and the NHS clearly have a more fundamental role in our lives, looking after our safety and health respectively. However, apart from an unlucky minority, most of us do not have a daily relationship with them and the work they do.

Realistically, and unglamorous as it sounds, your local council has a direct influence on a great number of the things we see and do every day and consequently it has a huge cumulative effect on our daily lives. Not all public services are a matter of life and death; many of them are about the daily activities of life and so they are extremely important to all of us on a very practical level.

Despite this day-to-day contact that most people have with their local council (whether direct or indirect) very few of us have an understanding of how local authorities actually work and even fewer take the opportunity to

4

become actively involved in how their local public services are run. So, in order to set the scene for the rest of the book, I thought it worthwhile to take a short time to go through the what, where, how and who of local councils. My apologies to readers who are already familiar with the internal machinations of their local town hall but it will be something of a whistle stop tour.

There are over 400 local authorities in the UK employing hundreds of thousands of staff. One council or another covers every square inch of the UK, which means that every resident is represented by one of the several thousand councillors.

Councils deliver a range of services from the familiar to the more surprising. Everyone knows that their bins are emptied by town hall teams but, in addition to this, many local councils are responsible for managing the following:

• Education – from employing teachers to ensuring the smooth running of schools.

• Social care – from protecting children at risk of being abused to caring for vulnerable older people.

• Environment – from cleaning the streets and ensuring that the roads are lit and maintained through to public health and trading standards.

• Leisure – provision of leisure centres, playgrounds, museums, art galleries and parks.

• Planning – controlling all building developments from conservatories to shopping centres and housing estates.

There are literally a hundred other services that are run by the council. All are aimed at helping local residents by improving the area in which they live and making sure that they can go about their day to day lives easily and in safety. Well, that's how the theory goes anyway.

In the majority of local authority areas the council is one of the biggest (if not the biggest) single employer. The average council employs several thousand people, which means that few private companies can compete by sheer weight of numbers. Like many other organisations of a comparable size local councils are structured in a traditional hierarchy; a Chief Executive sits at the top supported by a team of service directors each responsible for their specific area (Children's Services, Environment, Finance or whatever) with all their staff working within specific departments under each service head. Different to private businesses, however, is the existence of the elected councillors.

The role of elected councillors is hard to define in practice. I have devoted an entire chapter to some of the problems with the current system but at this stage the best analogy I have seen describes the elected members as the equivalent of shareholders in private companies. Working in collaboration with the officers, they are there to oversee the direction of the council and to ensure that what they want is implemented effectively. In short, the officers do the doing with elected members leading things by supporting, guiding and directing.

Every council works slightly differently but most of them have a ruling party that is voted into power at the local elections. Like the national government, the 'successful' party is able to set the direction for their local area; they decide on the major policies, what the priorities will be and so on. These elected councillors or 'members' are the local equivalent of MPs and get voted in (or out) on a four yearly election cycle.

In addition to the politicians every council has its own council officers employed and paid directly from the public purse. These are the local equivalent of civil servants – interviewed for their jobs and performing their huge range of functions from bin man and cleaner through to chief executives. These staff number in their hundreds even in the smaller authorities.

The theory is that even though power may shift between different political parties every so often that the officers manage the day-to-day running of the council through thick and thin. In practice many councils see a constant struggle between councillors and officers to establish exactly who is in charge of what. Councillors often have to fight to get real answers from officers who may agree with each other beforehand exactly what and how much the politicians really need to be told about a specific subject. Councillors on the other hand have been known to ask officers for the full facts, be told them, only to respond by asking for different ones as those facts don't really suit the decision that they want to make.

Financial management is a key part of the average council, as we shall see, and most local authorities are funded in the same basic way. Money raised from Council Tax contributions, a central government grant, and any other income streams such as fines and charges are combined together and then split down into budgets for each particular service. So, the Head of Children's Service is 'given' a budget of £x million to run all the appropriate services; the Head of Highways is given £y million and so on and so forth across the board.

In summary, that's the shape of local government. Something of a simplified view but as you make your way through the book you will see that all this is just the tip of the iceberg in understanding how things really operate.

3. Cottage Industries

"I had assumed that bullying was something the pupils did to each other but nowadays the adults feel free to get involved as well. I struggle with this concept and can't help thinking that any adult who feels they are being bullied by another adult probably ought to be. Lots of people need a kick up the backside now and again and a good boss has traditionally been the one to provide it. Unfortunately this is now called 'bullying'."

– Frank Chalk

Some years ago virtually every company and public sector organisation in Britain switched from having a 'personnel department' to having a 'human resources team'. I would guess that very little changed except perhaps, the name that appeared on the office door. In the public sector, and more specifically in the world of the local council, this change coincided with a real shift in the power that HR wielded in the town hall.

None of the 400-odd councils in the country could operate without HR. That, at least, is what the many HR officers would have you believe. I'm sure there are many so-called support services in both the public and private sector that would like their organisations to believe the same. The most worrying thing about HR in the town hall is that management actually agrees that HR are best placed to help them run each and every single department.

The role of HR, as I understand it, is – and should be – to assist the front line services in any staff related issues: recruitment, grievances, training and so on. And when you read what it says on the tin (or the HR Service Plan at least) that is what they say they do. However, the influence of HR seems to pervade a vast number of the decisions made across your bought-and-paid-for council services.

Doing what's right, or doing what's RIGHT

Very little in the bubble of HR seems to make sense in a world of practicalities and common sense. But council managers seem to hold HR advice in such high esteem that it affects a vast number of decisions throughout the town hall.

Take, for example, the simple and straightforward issue of recruitment. In the good old days, of course, things were easy. The perception was that managers could just drag in anyone off the street and if their face fitted they got the job. Secretaries were selected for how they looked in a low-cut blouse and a short skirt, fellow managers were chosen by which golf club they belonged to and the tea boy was chosen because he was the son of your neighbours and had 'always been a good lad'. To some extent this perception might not be a million miles away from the truth. However, at the same time, there were also plenty of managers who selected people for jobs based simply on their ability.

Since those days we have moved on and things are now a little fairer in the jobs market; vacancies need to be advertised, the recruitment process needs to be open and transparent and, of course, the employer must avoid discrimination at all costs. There is now legislation at a national level that, theoretically, applies to every company, council and statutory organisation in the country. As you'd expect, private companies adopt a pragmatic view of employment law and manage to find a largely workable system that may well annoy those who still have to jump through various hoops but at least satisfies the law and, more importantly, keeps the wasted time and effort completing paperwork to a reasonable minimum. This is because money spent on the pointless bits of the recruitment process is money lost from the annual profits.

Councils being councils have adopted a different approach to the whole process of recruiting staff. They have swallowed the employment regulations hook, line and sinker. Being a public service, councils naturally see themselves as caring, sharing employers and, as such, must go the extra mile when adopting any legislation around staff management.

My current employers have an incredibly laborious and extensive set of rules for all managers when they recruit new employees. No longer are we allowed to just put an advert in the paper, see who applies and pick the best candidate. As is their wont HR have produced a guidance manual (running to thirty-two pages) in my council, a dozen forms to be completed throughout the process and an internal training programme for all managers to ensure that they stick to the rules at all times.

This bureaucratic approach makes at least a degree of sense in principle, but in practice it becomes a cumbersome and over-elaborate system. According to our own HR department the whole recruitment process takes, on average, twenty-two weeks! That's nearly half a year to recruit someone into a post; if this is a model of efficiency then I worry about what an inefficient way of recruiting someone looks like. I hesitate to say how much time is wasted by managers putting numbers in the right column, writing checklists and double checking every last detail but a conservative estimate would suggest for each post that upwards of fifty staff hours are spent form filling and servicing the bureaucracy machine. While recruitment is probably one of the most important things that any organisation does, these hours are not spent talking to recruits, having positive and wide ranging discussions about the direction of the organisation and ensuring the right person is employed.

While every step in the process and every form that is filled in can undoubtedly be justified and explained, when an organisation has to go through this process several hundred or even a thousand times a year the indirect cost starts to look downright wasteful. Managers who should be concentrating on running front line services end up spending time ticking boxes to satisfy systems that have been developed and implemented by the organisation itself and are policed by a unit that is, theoretically, meant to make things more straightforward.

A streamlined approach does not, however, create work in HR and so it is not something that will ever be developed by a unit that wants to cement its place in an organisation. HR is not a support service that helps the average manager to navigate the maze of employment law. No, it is a strictly hands-off service. The people who work in HR do not help with the practicalities of employment, they don't work with staff to get issues sorted out, but have become policing agents that simply tell managers what they should be doing rather than doing it themselves.

Even more worryingly, HR doesn't seem to be very good at the policing role they have given themselves. When talking to one of my colleagues about the staff in his service he described the way that each individual had been recruited; a number had gone through the correct HR procedure but about 50% had literally been brought in off the street – a mixture of friends of friends, boyfriends of existing staff, neighbours of the head of service – you name it, every possible qualification was represented except the most important one: whether they were the best person for the job. But all the right forms had been filled in so officially there was no problem.

So if HR struggle to perform effectively in their policing role and some managers are able to ride rough shod over their systems then something must be wrong somewhere. We are left in the position where conscientious managers follow the rules no matter how ridiculous, and others who ignore them and do what they want anyway. Yet senior management does not seem to see these double standards, or the waste introduced by implementing more and more controls. More rules do not bring people into line, they simply mean the conscientious have to fight the system harder and harder each day and the others just do what they want.

This bureaucratic model doesn't just stop with the recruitment process. It is supplemented with grievance procedures, staff development, managing conflict, bullying and harassment, staff appraisal, the list goes on. All these issues need forms, paperwork, policies, and monitoring, making the system more and more bloated. The biggest growth area in councils seems to be in HR. However, instead of senior management questioning this and asking how we have reached such a position we continue to add more and more systems to 'safeguard' our staff and HR has become more and more remote from the actual frontline people whom they are there to support.

The training that is delivered to managers in order for them to understand all this extra paperwork means that they must take time out from their respective jobs to attend. Not only that, but the training has become an industry in its own right. To deliver all these courses we employ a full time training unit and a team of administrators who coordinate the bookings, organise the venues, and make sure the tea and biscuits are paid for etc. And, believe it or not, HR charges each service for their time!

The HR team have carved out a fantastic cottage industry. In the interest of offering value for money our HR team have been encouraged to quantify the cost of the courses they deliver and to charge departments for them. In fact HR has the business model to end all business models: they get to create policies and procedures that senior management then implement as corporate requirements that must be followed by everyone. Each department is told it *must* train all staff; HR then offer the services a course for £x and, finally, services are told that the only training provider they can use is HR. The term 'over a barrel' springs to mind.

The HR team who have created the policies fill their days by telling all the staff in the authority what the policy is and what they need to do to follow it properly. They then get to police things to make sure that the rules are followed, jumping on the conscientious who dare to fill out a form incorrectly whilst ignoring those who are just plain bad managers (the ones who recruit off the street) because they are too much work to deal with.

On top of this they don't actually have to deal with any complex HR issues directly; they tell managers how to deal with them and, rather than being supportive, they can just stand back and watch from the sidelines. The last piece of the jigsaw is complete when HR report at the end of the year that they have had an extremely successful year and have 'made' thousands of pounds from the fantastic courses they have provided.

Playing the System

"Several years ago our HR team devised a brand new system that would allow staff who felt that they were the victims of bad-treatment, harassment or bullying to complete a new form to report their worries so that HR could investigate it and take action if necessary. Within minutes of HR giving their briefing to staff one of our operatives blustered into the office and demanded eight copies of the new form. He duly returned all of these the next day, fully completed. There was one form written about every single manager in the whole service stating that each one of us had treated him with disrespect and were harassing him. It took nearly six months of stress, union meetings and hard work to investigate every single allegation. Not a single one was upheld and the operative later simply said, 'Well it's taught you lot not to f–k with me!'"

Beyond the bizarre bureaucracy and work creation that seems to pervade HR I have another major concern that the public are probably aware of. That is people who play the system. The above example is one of many that I might have used to show how vexatious reporting, troublemaking, and general Mickey-taking occurs in all the councils where I have worked. The pendulum has most certainly swung in favour of those staff in the council who feel the world owes them a living.

Working for the council brings all sorts of additional benefits that aren't generally available outside the public sector, at least not to the same extent anyway. From maternity leave and sickness to flexi-time and special leave every member of staff in every council in the country is in a very lucky position in terms of their employment rights. We'll not even touch on the local government pension scheme here as that could fill a book all on its own.

These fringe benefits are not bad things in themselves. Which of us could honestly say that we would turn down any one of them if offered? However, for every positive there is a negative; there are always those who abuse the system. These kinds of people exist in every organisation – people who borrow the office stationery, who slope off early each day, who pull sickies at every available opportunity. The council, however, has created a system where, far from weeding these people out and dealing with them properly, it propagates a culture where everyone can and many do take advantage.

Take sick leave as an example. Most private companies offer some degree of sick pay and their overriding desire is to get the employee back to work as soon as possible. If someone isn't attending then their work needs covering, which costs money, so it is in the best interest of the company to get them back. In order to achieve this, the company might offer attendance bonuses or strictly limited sick pay benefits.

Your town hall officials approach it slightly differently. They offer full sick pay for six months and only then reduce it to half pay. But if the person in question is able to attend work for a day or two after their six months is up the system is reset and they are allowed to go off for another six months on full pay. Eventually the council get a bit annoyed at this and after the third or fourth time this happens they actually do something. Not by getting rid of the person, you understand – that might be a bit risky and open the council up to accusations of being bad employers or even the much feared tribunal. No, far better to have a nice sit down and a bit of a chat to see what the council can do to better support the employee in question. After the implementation of a plan to help the individual back to work and various review meetings the person might actually come back to work, perhaps on reduced hours, perhaps on lighter duties. Either way they have cost the taxpayer thousands upon thousands of pounds.

One operative I worked with at my last local authority

had been playing the system for nearly four years. During that time he had worked for perhaps six weeks in total but the management was not able to do a thing to get him back to work. The authority was finally able to shed the deadwood but not before having paid out nearly £100,000 in wages for virtually no work, as well as a lump sum early retirement package.

The sheer scale of this employee-friendly culture is mind-boggling. Virtually every service I have worked for has had people like this who swing the lead. Now I'm not saying that some people don't need help and support when they are genuinely ill but these people are massively outnumbered by those who milk the system. Sickness levels in councils are twice what they are in the private sector. This is not because public sector workers are genetically weaker and more prone to illness, it's simply because the systems allow more people to get away with it.

With so many benefits coming to council employees it is little wonder that, despite the supposedly poor pay and perceived low status, people very rarely (if ever) leave the cosseted environment of the town hall. Would you? And as for the council actually getting rid of people, well on that note I'm afraid to say that everything you may have heard about the impossible job councils have in getting rid of staff is absolutely true.

During my twenty or so years in councils around the country I have only ever experienced a couple of people even coming close to being sacked. The first person's offence was to distribute internet pornography and to sell pirated DVDs whilst at work. I suppose even the most lily-livered council would hesitate to keep hold of him. Having said this even that incident was not exactly an outstanding example of swift justice. Despite being caught red-handed in the act, as it were, it took nearly six months whilst he was suspended on full pay just to arrange a meeting between him, his union rep and the management.

Following this meeting he decided that discretion was the better part of valour and he handed his notice in. At least it saved another six months of paperwork, meetings, appeals, and money.

The second instance involved a colleague of mine who was the investigating officer in an alleged incident of misconduct. Rather unbelievably one of the authority's grass cutters was accused of taking payment to cut the grass at private companies' premises. He had been caught in the act by his manager and had been immediately suspended on full pay for misuse of council equipment and taking payment for work carried out whilst on duty. When interviewed over the incident by the investigating officer the operative admitted everything. On this evidence the head of service was able to dismiss the man in question immediately. Sadly, after this the employment machine shuddered into gear. A more senior union rep was brought in and the case went to full appeal. This basically meant that the head of service had to present his case to a panel of councillors who formed the appeals committee. In this case, despite the fact his manager caught him and that he had admitted to taking money, the appeals panel felt that there was not enough evidence against him and that he should be reinstated immediately. As a result the head of service was made to feel impotent and ineffective; the manager of the operative had to go back to supervising a man who knew that he could get away with whatever he wanted and the operative's colleagues were all well aware that murder had well and truly been got away with.

Surely both these cases do little to create an environment where staff develop respect for the organisation they work for and the work shy are fearful of being found out. Indeed, these examples just typify why so many people continue to get away with so much. If we struggle so hard to get rid of the genuine thieves and problem makers, what chance does an organisation have of dealing with those who are just lazy or playing the system?

"It is highly improbable that the bureaucrat will put his life on the line. It is absolutely impossible that he'll put his job on the line."

– Anon

Joining the council has a number of extra fringe benefits for people who, shall we say, are getting a job for less than genuine reasons. These benefits go far beyond the pension, flexi-time and generally lax environment for those who want to fill their boots up. Councils are an attraction for the dead, the lame and the lazy. However, once recruited everyone in the council has a fantastic opportunity to climb aboard the proverbial gravy train. And trust me – virtually everyone takes their opportunity in one way or another.

Take for example one gentleman I worked with some years ago. He was one of those rare commodities in the council: a front line worker. Dave had worked in a variety of jobs which included being a bin man and a street cleaner. However, when I knew him he had cornered the market in driving sweeper lorries. Dave was one of only a handful of lads who knew how to drive the machines and who had knowledge of the routes around the district. He knew his skills were in short supply and in combination with our toothless approach to staff management he had us over a barrel.

Dave was the sort of man who made the most of his situation. I honestly lost track of the number of times that Dave was caught by myself or one the department's managers either sleeping in his cab in a local lay-by or clocking on at a weekend and disappearing home until it was clocking off time. The council, being the council, turned a blind eye and formal warnings were ignored and so on. This is the culture for many individuals within the town hall and while many officers work hard it seems that many more take advantage at every available opportunity. An interesting follow up for Dave and the thing that shocked me more than anything was when I found out how much money he earned from his job. While I can't knock the work that the front-line lads do I did raise an eyebrow when an annual wage of £48,000 flagged up on our system for Dave. That wasn't unusual; over the ten years that we had the records for he had 'earned' half a million pounds based largely, it seemed, on spurious overtime claims and forty winks in the cab.

Dave wasn't alone in his approach to work but he was certainly the king of the hill when it came to making overtime claims. The culture of milking the system at every available opportunity continues to exist throughout councils up and down the country. From arranging meetings as far away as possible in order to claim the maximum permitted mileage to putting on events at a weekend to ensure that you get double time for attending. I am sure this goes on in the private sector, but the private sector workers are screwing over the shareholders; council workers are screwing over every single taxpayer.

I have talked previously about the role of HR in promulgating this culture and I shall speak in more detail about the lack of management that allows it to continue. However, every single member of staff working in a town hall who milks the system makes their own decision to do so. Let's not only blame the system; people make individual choices about what they claim, how they work and how much effort they put in. Everyone involved is an adult and should know better.

Almost all the jobs I've had in local government could be done (to the job description at least) in about half the hours per week on the contract. I suspect this is not unique to those jobs I have had and that the majority fall into this category. To me this means there are several types of people working in the council:

- Those who don't realise/have the skills to realise this and somehow contrive to fill their days through ineptitude and even think they are overworked.
- Those who do realise/have the skills to do the minimum and take the Mick for the remaining time.
- Those who realise and choose to do more and ignore demarcation lines and their job description.

It would be interesting to see which group people think they belong to. I haven't had the time or inclination to survey a cross section of my colleagues but it doesn't take a rocket scientist to work out that a vast majority sit in the first two groups. This is no doubt mirrored to a greater or lesser extent in the private sector but again this is public money; people should be busting their proverbial gut to deliver good value for money. But I feel I may be in a minority on that one, and I certainly wouldn't dream of airing that sentiment in my office.

The culture of the public sector has created a situation where hard work and dedication isn't always rewarded. Those who bullshit do best. Those who don't work hide too easily. Those who don't make decisions rise up the ranks. And those in the middle just get lost in a quagmire of bureaucracy.

Some council staff are genuine and want to see improvement to the system and do all they can. A larger number of staff are just honest people turning up to work and doing their job – It's not their fault they are employed doing the wrong thing. But there are a significant number of council staff who are the real problem. These are often senior managers who can actually really make a difference and don't. These are the people who seem to enjoy the system, benefit from it, and can see no other way. Essentially they just don't see any need for change.

My final point on the gravy train is around the length of time that people take advantage of it. Hardly a month goes by in my authority without some staff member or another being promoted in the internal magazine as receiving an award for long service. Ten years of service is a drop in the ocean; thirty or forty years are more the norm. While I'm impressed by these people's longevity, I genuinely I have to question whether councils are best served by people who have been in what is often the same post for such an unbelievable period of time. Some would suggest that it is great to have such extensive experience and knowledge within an organisation.

In fact to take this point a stage further I would question whether these individuals who have become part of the town hall furniture actually are that experienced. These people don't have twenty years of hard-fought experience; they have one year of experience repeated twenty times and have often learnt little or nothing along the way.

Undue Influence

When recruiting to one post in my department that had been funded by a generous government grant a couple of years ago I went through the compulsory rigmarole of getting permission, advertising the post, receiving a dozen or so application forms and short-listing. I was then contacted by someone in HR who informed me that there was someone on the internal redeployment list (that is people who are close to the end of their contract with the council and must be considered for a new post in the authority at any expense) whom I had to interview before everyone else who had applied. Our employee friendly policies meant that we got people's hopes up of securing a new job in the local area and then simply said, "Sorry, we can't interview you yet, there's someone in the council who's more important to interview first."

So, a colleague, an HR representative, and myself interviewed the internal candidate.

Interviews are very prescriptive. Each person being interviewed receives a score out of a hundred by the end of the process. Before the interview takes place the panel agree a baseline score that the successful candidate must reach as a minimum. Whoever scores the highest on the combined total from each panellist then gets the job, provided they have scored higher than the benchmark. (That's right, the complex business of assessing personal attributes, understanding team dynamics and analysing an individual's skills has come down to putting a number in a box and then deciding which number is bigger.)

We set the benchmark for this job at 70%, meaning that anyone below that mark couldn't get the job. We interviewed the woman in question and scored her at somewhere just over 50%. Nice though she was, she just wasn't suitable for the job. This was something both my colleague and myself agreed upon. However, the following day the HR manager contacted us. We were told that because the candidate had met the necessary benchmark they must be offered the job. Despite our protestations we were presented with a new rule from HR.

"Any redeployee who scores within 80% of a benchmark must be offered the job."

This was new to me and the principle certainly concerned me.

On this one HR would not be moved, they insisted that despite the candidate not being suitable for the job and scoring significantly below the benchmark that we had set, according to their rules she must be employed against the wishes of the managers of the service. Our own head of service took this further, appealed the decision, argued and cajoled, but HR would not be budged. In fairness to them, they did add one additional statement. They said that our team could refuse to employ her but that if the candidate was not employed by us and decided to take it to tribunal then our department would not receive the support of HR in court and we would be on our own.

You won't be surprised to learn that we ended up employing the woman in question. The result was that morale in our department hit rock bottom as a member of staff who had neither the skills nor experience to do the job, was employed. On speaking to her she told me that she was not particularly bothered about getting the job but HR had put her forward and it was better than being out of work. In fairness to her she tried her very best to carry out the work to a good standard and she performed as well as could have been expected.

So what did the system provide in this instance? A dozen members of the public had applied for a job that they stood no chance of getting, for reasons completely out of their control; a team were forced to employ an individual they didn't feel was suitable; a new staff member started in a team where, in all honesty, things were against her from the outset; and a situation where the people in charge of the service were overruled, not for purposes to serve the greater good of the electorate but to ensure that HR policies and internal staff in other areas are satisfied over and above anything else.

To Buy or Not to Buy

"The hate crime unit 'deals with' hate crime in a democratic sense only; it sends threatening forms advising me of (police) force policy, I

*tick some boxes and return them. When it comes to ACTUALLY
dealing with hate crime, and catching offenders, that's MY job... by
this method, every front line officer can keep another person in a job
who would otherwise be out of work."*

– PC David Copperfield

Some of you (particularly those of you who work in
HR) may be thinking that I have been a little harsh. As
with many things within the council there are some good
people working in HR. That doesn't mean that the system
isn't wrong though and HR represents just one of many
services at the town hall which are set up with a role to
support the frontline delivery of services but end up
becoming their very own 'cottage industry', i.e. they
employ people to service its own continuation. In other
words, they do little to deliver anything useful to the
average resident.

Another one of my particular bugbears is the approach
town halls have towards procurement – a fancy word for
buying stuff. In all the authorities I have worked in the
procurement team have developed their own job creation
cottage industry.

In the private companies I have worked for we have
invariably had a separate buying team. This team would be
responsible not necessarily for buying every bottle of
Tippex and roll of Sellotape but rather for sourcing the
best possible price for chemicals, raw materials, shipment
containers, pallets or whatever was needed to carry out the
business. You may think that a council procurement team
might work in the same way, building relationships with
suppliers, researching the markets to get the best prices
and ensuring that the organisation spends as little as
possible on the best quality materials and services.

Unfortunately this isn't quite the way it works. Our
current procurement team are strictly hands off and don't

actually buy anything; like HR they are there simply to advise on 'best practice'. In other words, they are there to create systems, frameworks and paperwork and then ensure that every person in the council follows the proper procedure and, just like HR, woe betide anyone caught using their own initiative.

In the interest of protecting public money and to ensure that 'backhanders' to council officials from private companies are a thing of the past procurement rules were changed nationally. This meant that councils were presented with another fantastic opportunity to employ more people to make a straightforward process, like buying materials and services, as complicated as humanly possible.

Now I can see the sense in ensuring that when council employees purchase something they obtain a number of quotes, because it helps to ensure that the best price is obtained. However, surely this is just an example of the common sense that all employees should be showing anyway? Does it really need a team of internal enforcers that just costs us all extra money and who don't actually save any money?

The best (or worst) bit of the procurement process is the system that has to be followed for larger purchases (those over a few thousand pounds). No one could argue that large outlays of cash need to be effectively managed by councils but I would question whether the process that has been put in place provides either an effective use of time or delivers good value for money. Further I'd also query whether it stops the unscrupulous managers who ignore the regulations for less than genuine reasons.

Quite recently a colleague of mine was in a position to buy in the services of a recruitment agency to find children's crèche and nursery staff. The contract was a large one and involved nurseries across four neighbouring local authorities. Three of the authorities had already been through their own processes and had opted for one particular company across all their areas. So what do you think was our approach?

A) See the opportunity to join in with the larger contract and negotiate a deal for ourselves through our own expert buyers and negotiators.

Or

B) Waste time, staff hours and valuable resources to write a forty-page tender specification, spend money advertising the potential contract, use administration staff to collate the responses, waste a full day of four staff members' time carrying out interviews with providers, spend another day carrying out second-round interviews, devise a five-page scoring checklist and finally award the contract to the company that had the contract in the three neighbouring authorities anyway. Then carry out an added bit of administration that would take the whole process over the five-month mark for completion and so cause my colleague, who has to manage the whole process (rather than the procurement team), weeks and weeks of unnecessary work whilst also trying to run his service on a daily basis.

If any of you said 'B' then you win a goldfish.

Now the procurement experts amongst you will point out that option B) is a legal requirement. On that point I partly agree. However, the national legislation is down to local councils to interpret and they invariably ensure that this favours the most bureaucratic and labour-intensive approach possible. I'm all for openness and transparency in buying things but I question whether the cottage industry of procurement actually presents value for money.

When you consider the actual cost of procurement it is bizarre that anyone would consider this the best approach. A council procurement team has numerous full time staff that need paying for, despite the fact that they do little more than offer advice. Managers elsewhere in the council are the ones who actually spend time doing the purchasing at the expense of spending time managing their services and the paperwork and administration exponentially increases the time and effort required to get the job done. Still, at least all the boxes are ticked.

Fundamentally I would even ask whether the final price to supply the goods in question is actually the best one possible. Even if you don't add in the 'hidden costs' described above (which councils never do when they proclaim their latest success in sealing a new contract) the prices the council pay are just too much. I have worked with some fantastic buyers in my brief foray in the private sector who seem able to negotiate amazing deals, given the right flexibility to source suppliers. This includes, where necessary, the authority to threaten to cancel contracts. The key word to getting a good price, then, is 'negotiation'. Sadly, because the council are now so transparent with their deals, the price first quoted by a company is the price that is invariably accepted (despite claims to the contrary); there is no talking, no discussion and no negotiating. A good buyer is worth their weight in gold to a private company, but in your average town hall the skill of artful negotiation seems to have gone the same way as the dodo.

Tax DOES have to be Taxing

You may (or may not) be surprised to learn that councils have to pay themselves council tax on their own properties. The justification for this being that if every other building in a local authority area has to pay it then so should all the council buildings. You can't argue with the logic I suppose.

What you might want to argue with is the way that the system works on this one. Given that the annual budget for the council is collated centrally at the start of the year and divvied out to its various departments you may think that this would be the ideal opportunity for the Council Tax department to keep its share of the pot, or at least for the Council Tax department column to have the appropriate numbers added in. While this may be the case in some councils, the ones I have worked in decided a lengthier alternative would be much better. They have created their own cottage industry of invoicing and administrating.

The department responsible for managing each and every council building actually receives a council tax bill, just like the average resident does, from their very own colleagues. Not a big deal in itself but when you consider that most authorities operate swimming pools, care homes, cemetery chapels and office buildings across their area this might involve a significant number of council tax bills. All of these services need someone to raise the bill, someone to send it out, someone in each department to sign off the bill, someone else to arrange a transfer of funds from one account code to another, someone else to chase up the department in question if things aren't paid, and so it goes on. This is all the same pot of money being swished around from one room in the town hall to another. Why does it need all this? Why are we paying our own staff to pay ourselves our own money?

On the scale of things perhaps I am being a little pedantic picking on this particular example. Fifty or sixty extra pieces of paperwork is not much within the these paper-based leviathan councils, but it does demonstrate yet another example of doing things just for the sake of it because no one really understands that when you add up all these little bits they equal a vast amount of waste. I am sure there are a hundred similar examples in private companies, but they aren't spending public money. Being selfish, it also gives me an opportunity to relate one story resulting from these bills.

When managing one particular service I had a number of buildings under my control. One of these equated to a lunch cabin for some of the grounds maintenance staff in a local park. For some reason this building was council tax rated (presumably because at some time in the past it was a habitable property!). Being new and naive at the time I was extremely surprised when a council tax bill plopped on my desk for the property in question. Undaunted by my own naivety, I gave it the appropriate level of attention and ignored it completely and put it down to a mistake by the tax office (I apologise now for my thoughtless dereliction of duty). Several weeks later I received a copy of the same bill but this time it was in an attractive scarlet colour that demanded payment of the bill or court action would be taken. Thinking that this couldn't be a serious threat I contacted the department in question only to be told in no uncertain terms that I would most certainly be taken to court and that this was no idle threat. After I'd stopped laughing I spoke to my manager and asked a) whether this was for real and b) whether this was really the most efficient way of running a professional organisation. Sadly both my manager and I chickened out from calling our colleague's bluff and decided to transfer the necessary money over. This was a shame as I was hoping to see a notice somewhere in the local newspaper's court pages about us taking ourselves to court. It's a pity that the town's public never got to see that little gem. In fairness the lady I spoke to said that the council tax office never loses in court. In her defence if we'd taken ourselves on, and given that we'd have been on *both* sides in front of the magistrate I'm pretty confident that 'the council' would have won in court one way or another.

The Diversity Diversion

"Britons are now officially divided into 15 species and 65 sub-species according to their ethnicity. This data is collected by all public sector bodies and is monitored by diversity officers in order to rid us all of racial inequality once and for all."

– Ross Clark

One of my favourite cottage industries (and I promise the last one I'll speak about for now) that you will find in most councils is the diversity unit. It is packaged under a variety of different guises but its role is invariably the same – to monitor activity, projects and processes in the town hall to ensure that they are fair to all. These equality police have the remit to demand quite a lot from council employees. Yet every extra piece of work that they expect from each member of staff costs you, the taxpayer, money, and detracts from the day job.

In one council I worked at the diversity team sent out a directive saying that because they had purchased some new computer software it must now be 'populated'. Essentially, this meant that every department, service and team had to give examples of what had been done over the previous twelve months to promote diversity in their work.

However inane and pointless you may think that this exercise was, this is nothing when you start to understand the scale of the whole thing. We were told (and a three-line whip backed it up) that the computer system needed updating within three months to be in line with our corporate pledge (whatever that means). At the time our own service manager had caught the diversity bug in rather a worrying way and so we were forced to embrace the system wholeheartedly. This must have cost our team alone more than a week's worth of staff hours in the first month alone. If just half of all the other teams followed the same approach then more than a year's worth of wages were spent on this scheme.

The software was split into a variety of different sections, each of which asked questions on what we had done to promote gender equality in our day-to-day work, what plans we had to promote age related diversity in our long term strategy, what complaints had been received about racial discrimination, and so the list went on. Eight members of our team huddled round a computer screen completing the necessary boxes on the diversity team's new system. Each part of the system needed discussion, agreement, copious note-taking and eventual writing up of all the key points to satisfy the diversity police.

Three or four months later, once all the services had sent through their information, the diversity team thanked everyone involved for their hard work. I imagine that the exact scale of the operation was never fully appreciated. But then we were told that, following discussions by the corporate management team, the system was no longer going to be used and that a new system would be introduced in the near future. Sadly – if that's the right word – all the work was lost and nothing further was ever seen or heard of it.

While of course this example represents a waste of your council tax money and staff-time it is the environment that is created which is of greater concern. Every piece of work, every project and even every report that is written must explain and justify its role not just in terms of what results it will achieve (cleaner streets, better educated kids, or whatever) but how it satisfies the necessary rules and regulations around equality. Few could argue that services don't need to be inclusive but I genuinely doubt whether this obsession for equality really achieves what it sets out to do. It gives managers, staff and local residents more hoops to jump through and boxes to tick but it doesn't deal with any of the issues that actually matter.

"If the Commission for Racial Equality cease finding evidence of racism, we don't really need them anymore and they'll all have to pack up and go find other jobs."

– PC David Copperfield

The fight for diversity in the town hall creates quite a bizarre situation where the trump card of 'this is a diversity issue' is played by all those staff who want to cause maximum disruption for minimum effort. In one authority where I worked for a brief period of time a member of staff was caught up in an office switch around. She'd previously had the privilege of her own office for several years despite the fact that it was not necessarily needed for her job role and that she'd had it a bit cushy for quite a long time. The office move basically meant that she'd have to mix in with everyone else in a shared office in the new building.

Despite the usual grumbles when any team are forced to switch locations the team accepted the move and everything was arranged for the new venue. However, the woman who'd had her own office decided not to play so nicely and rather than accepting it graciously (or at the very least taking the issue further based solely on the office) instead reported to senior management that she was being thrown out of her office due to the fact that she was black.

Without fully understanding the senior management psyche at that time I am unable to confirm whether or not the collective might of the town hall had indeed planned and conspired to manufacture an unnecessary departmental relocation, impacting on about thirty staff, with the sole intention of getting one individual black manager out of her office. I somehow doubt it, partly because very few people are actually that racist, and partly because management simply isn't that organised.

Perhaps I'm naive though and, in reality, the authority really was that bigoted and devious. What I can confirm is that after three months the office move hadn't taken place, the equality team were investigating allegations of racism and dozens of staff hours had been wasted on a fruitless search for evidence of a cover-up. Now if one trump card can be played with such nonchalant complacency and create such a quagmire, imagine what someone with a real sense of menace could achieve in this environment of political correctness.

Council Services You Didn't Know You Had

While not exactly falling under the heading of cottage industries I couldn't end this chapter without making some mention of the services that councils provide that will, hopefully, make the casual reader think a little more about the role of their town hall officials. As well as what you might term 'standard' services, highlighted in the earlier chapters, many councils operate a variety of non-standard services. This basically means that some manager, sat in an office somewhere, thinks that he's got a quiet few months ahead of him and perhaps he should be seen to be doing something. So he comes up with a hare-brained scheme to look busy and to make the council look like it is doing plenty to support their local communities. Below are just a few of my particular favourites. I promise to move on after you've looked at these but as you read down the list I ask you just to consider whether, if given the choice, these are services that you would like delivered by your own council and using money from your council tax. All the examples are real, all use council tax funding or resources to run (e.g.

staff, offices etc.). They are not all 'distinct' departments but all of them are the responsibility of one team or another.

St Patrick's Day Celebration Event – there is many a time that I've been out to celebrate St Patrick's Day; I'm not Irish and have no Irish ancestry but still I go. I have never felt the need for a council run celebration to complement the promotions on at Ye Olde Scruffy Murphy's Inn, nor have I felt that my tax money should be spent by people sat in a meeting room discussing what the local populous might enjoy to mark the annual saint's day (of another country).

Resilience Team – this council-based service produces leaflets and web-based advice on the items that the general populous should keep in a natural disaster kit. I didn't feel the need to read on, even when I learnt that there was such a thing as a natural disaster kit and that it might save my life. For those of you out there that are fearful of earthquakes, volcanoes and tsunamis I apologise for my flippancy, but I am yet to be convinced that disaster survival tips are absolutely necessary from town hall officers.

Advice on Buying a Car – that's right, if *Autotrader*, *Top Gear* and every other possible resource for learning how to purchase an automobile don't quite do it for you, just contact your town hall and some helpful officer will give you their best advice on what colour car would best go with your eyes, or whether the latest Mercedes will depreciate more quickly than the equivalent model of BMW (or other prestige automobile).

Advice on Cloning – this was one of my favourites

when I found it and simply made me wonder which town hall was able to claim have an expert on the incredibly complex world of genetics and cell modification on their payroll. I couldn't help but be impressed that the particular council in question had 'Must have degree in biochemistry' on their recruitment advert.

Cooling Tower and Evaporative Condenser Registration – Really? What? I'm not expert enough to understand what on earth this involves but it sounds like fun. Please could any Cooling Tower and Condenser Evaporative Condenser Registration Officers out there contact me to explain it? I occasionally struggle to sleep at nights and would welcome the information to just send me off.

Manifestations of Japanese Knotweed – in fairness every morning when I leave the house my car struggles to get out of the drive due to the roaming manifestations of knotweed that curse our lovely neighbourhood. The local children are no longer allowed out alone and there have been several reports of small dogs disappearing in the area. I think the UN Task Force that has now been deployed have the problem under control, but at least the council have produced a leaflet to help out the local citizens.

Real Nappy Service – unfortunately this team of officers are not there to come round and change your baby and wash the resulting nappies. No this team is there to promote the use of real nappies as opposed to disposable ones. Whether or not you agree with the environmental benefit, we have to ask whether the average council in isolation has the ability or wherewithal to compete with the advertising budget of Pampers. And even if it does, isn't this a national campaign rather than one where council tax money is spent in two hundred plus councils separately?

Nutrition Task Force – I have a strange vision of a Lycra-clad armed response team bursting in on unsuspecting couch potatoes as they are about to tuck into their second kebab of the evening and who then promptly start force-feeding the startled individual steamed broccoli. I suspect, however, that this is more likely to be a team of office-based officers dreaming up new ways to market healthy eating in a programme that simply replicates what the NHS and National Government are already doing.

Sun Safety Campaign – does the council really need to spend time and money creating media campaigns, web pages etc. to tell its residents to slap on the sunscreen and not go out into Britain's invariably blistering summer sun?

High Hedges Legislation and Guidance – legislation *and* guidance on this one. It's a worry that there is national legislation on this particular political hot potato in the first place but that the town hall then feels the need to supplement this with their own leaflets and fact sheets just compounds things. All just to make sure that the *Leylandii* next door doesn't creep above the eight foot mark.

A Way Forward

This one is a tough cookie to crack. The various cottage industries in town halls up and down the land are so ingrained in the council structure that to strip them out would be the equivalent of Hercules cleaning the Augean Stables. And not every town hall has a nearby river that can be diverted so we need to find a solution elsewhere.

Council leaders' first step is to take a more active role

in deciding how legislation and guidance is implemented and not just accept the interpretation given by their advisors. Legislation is one thing and naturally needs adhering to; however, even within the confines of the law there are a variety of interpretations available. Take HR, for example. All organisations in this country operate under national employment law yet each one has very different rules for their employees. Town halls need to move away from interpretations that create new jobs for people and move towards approach that means front line services can get on with their jobs rather than having ridiculous hoops to jump through. In short, the mind-set needs to shift towards implementing legislation to an appropriate level rather than to the maximum possible. This means effectively being more hard-faced in the management of staff, where the knotty problem of redundancy is faced then every case needs looking at individually. Simply slotting people into supposedly similar posts by skewing benchmarks and rigging interviews cannot be acceptable. Where an individual proves themselves to be capable of changing role then of course it is fine. But to have just one approach where we find jobs for everyone has to be ultimately damaging to the organisation as a whole and so needs to stop. Turnover of staff, if managed properly, can be an incredibly valuable thing for any organisation and not allowing this to happen naturally achieves little positive for the wider community.

Similarly, when it comes to sick and maternity leave, however unpopular it will be, minimum legal requirements need to be the norm. Not going the extra mile for staff. Like many solutions in life this may be unpalatable for certain individuals but again it is a step in the right direction so that councils help themselves and their residents more. The benefits provided by council have been there so long that sadly they have become seen as a right rather a privilege. It is time to take away the child's security blanket and introduce them to the real world.

The dismissal of staff needs to be sharpened up too. No more loopholes and third, fourth and fifth chances for people. Councils need to be stronger in their whole approach to staff management. Sticking to initial decisions to get rid of a staff member of example is not a sign of blinkered pig-headedness; sometimes, just sometimes, it sends out the right message to everyone involved that the council will not be taken advantage of. Because taking advantage of the council is misuse of public money.

Away from the HR side and looking at the other support services we have looked at I understand that there are still hoops to be jumped through – such is procurement law. But where hoops do still need to be jumped through, there needs to be a move away from front line staff being forced to do the jumping. Currently these staff are given this extra work to do under the guise of 'front line staff know best'.

While this argument is fundamentally true – front line staff are meant to be good at their front line duties – they don't necessarily know or have the time or specific skills to find out what the best value is for supplies If I go out for a meal to a fancy restaurant I expect the chef to cook the food. I'd rather not be told that I know what food I like best so I should go into the kitchen and cook it myself while the chef sits nearby to advise and criticise as necessary from the sidelines.

Getting the right people doing the right job in this way does not mean a return to the bad old days of demarcation and an attitude of, "That's not my job." Far from it; it means that councils will have, amongst other things, a recruitment team that actually recruits people and a procurement team that actually procures things with support and advice from the services. Not such a radical system really.

Finally, council leaders need to examine every internal department and question whether it adds any value to the life of residents in their local area. Of course I accept that some services are what people might term a 'necessary evil', such as finance and HR, but if the department in question is running a cottage industry that residents don't benefit from then why on earth is it allowed to continue to operate in that way?

4. Culture Vultures

"I bought a doughnut and they gave me a receipt. I don't need a receipt for the doughnut. I give you money and you give me the doughnut, end of transaction. We don't need to bring ink and paper into this. I can't imagine a scenario that I would have to prove that I bought a doughnut. To a sceptical friend; don't even act like I didn't get that doughnut, I've got the documentation right here... it's in my file at home... under 'D'."

– Mitch Hedberg

The so-called 'culture' of working for particular organisations is something that management gurus are very keen on. From the culture of job insecurity and sacking people by text message that pervades the more poorly run private sector call centres to the background of bureaucracy and micro-management that seems to exist in every aspect of public sector organisations.

There are many public perceptions of what it is like to work at the town hall, and many of them, I have to say, are not a million miles away from the truth. Ken Dodd's comment at the start of the book is perhaps the most succinct way of summarising the general perceptions of the cushy lifestyle that exists in the town hall. All you have to do is read the message boards and internet forums that are hosted by campaigners or local newspapers to see that people are very cynical about what council workers really do for them.

Council culture is a huge area and, like many things I have written about, it could fill a book by itself. In researching this, though, I have encountered a number or articles that 'lift the lid' on working for councils up and down the country. Many of these confirm the worst suspicions of the public: that every council worker in the country sits at their desk all day, drinking tea, doing nothing and crossing off the hours until they can go home. While I can't deny that this situation certainly does exist, these articles don't delve deeply enough into what it really means to work for the council.

Rules, Rules, Rules

"Rules are for the obedience of fools and the guidance of wise men."

– Anon

One of the most overriding principles that exists in town halls – and one that frustrates most if not all members of the public at some point – is the one that simply states, "I'm sorry sir, those are the rules." This is the oft-cited Jobsworth attitude that has featured everywhere from *That's Life* in the 70s and 80s to a myriad of amusing websites today.

Sticking to the rules is probably the key tenet for all council officers. The huge advantage of following rules is that you can never be wrong. Well, on paper at least. Council employees are given the policy diktats – e.g. when in position A then take decision A. These standard rules become an 'absolute' that must be followed blindly no matter what the practicalities of the situation and create a complete lack of flexibility for the entire organisation.

One of the reasons that rules are followed so strictly, of course, is the sense of fear that the officer on the ground has. All the way through their training at the council it will have been drilled into them – that policy and rules are their guiding light, and that without these rules we would have nothing but anarchy. In short, policies and procedures are their safety net and best friend. In this culture of adherence there is little wonder that front line officers are in a position where, rather than making a common sense decision, they just go with what it says in the rule book.

The hundreds of Jobsworth examples that are reported in the media, where some poor citizen has been the victim of some ridiculous decision or another, will invariably prompt some council spokesperson to come out in defence of the system. Their defence is being something along the lines of, "An over-zealous worker interpreting things wrongly," (they daren't tell you that their workers are not allowed to interpret things at all) or, "Sorry, but that is the policy."

But these answers do not allow for – or fully explain – the culture that exists for staff when they are making every day decisions; that rules are there to be followed. It's clear and simple: don't follow them and it's your fault. This doesn't foster decision-making and flexibility, it fosters people managing by the book and removes any element of judgement being used. But if you follow the rules, however stupid they are, you know (it's official) you are right.

So this over-legislation and rule adherence removes an individual officer's discretion, it takes away their responsibility and makes it more likely that the excuse of 'the rules made me do it' will be rolled out.

"This just about sums up everything that is wrong with the bureaucratic mind. Think of a noble aim, come up with a solution which appears to lead in the right direction [rules] then enforce it in such a generic and pedantic fashion it ends up achieving exactly the opposite of what you set out to achieve."

– Ross Clark

The sense of fear among employees goes a little further though. Part of the reason why rules are followed so inflexibly is the worry of setting a precedent. This excuse is wheeled out so often you wouldn't believe it. One example of this, which I was involved in, concerned a sweet old dear who lived in one of the villages looked after by our council services. She'd lived in her house since god knows when and now struggled to get all the jobs done around the house. She didn't receive any support from our social services team though, because her neighbours and family looked after her and they helped to get most things done. Our service looked after her refuse collection and the rule at that time was that residents had to place their bins at the roadside in order to be collected by our operatives. The only exceptions to this rule were for those households where people were not able to physically get the bins off their property and to the roadside. This meant that the elderly and infirm were exempt from having to put out their own bins – so long as they were on the 'social services list'. If they were on the list then our bin lads could go into the property to collect the bins themselves. This was a reasonable ruling that largely made sense.

The lady in question, however, had never come to our attention before because a neighbour had always helped her put her bin out. Unfortunately, the neighbour had moved and the lady was in a predicament. She didn't want to ask her new neighbour to do it so she asked us for our help. The full bureaucratic machine kicked slowly into gear and she was asked to make alternative arrangements until a full assessment could be made of her needs by trained social services professionals. Sadly, depending on workloads, this could take up to two months. In the mean time she would have to use her Zimmer frame and do it herself, or else make alternative arrangements for as long as needed.

Admittedly this is a small thing but the lady had paid her way all through her life and was certainly not a burden on local services. She was in a position where she just wanted a little bit of extra support, which wouldn't really have made any major dents in local budgets, but these rules meant that she wasn't able to get it, at least not within a reasonable timescale. When the case was presented to my colleague who managed the bin rounds his immediate response was the predictable, "Well she can wait for the assessment like everyone else, I'm not setting a precedent for malingerers using our staff to do what they should be doing themselves. That's how the flood gates open." The implication being that she was taking advantage of the system and that if we helped her then, by definition, we'd have to help everyone.

It is this danger of setting a precedent that seems to petrify the average local authority manager. My understanding of 'setting a precedent' is that this can only be done in a court of law, and even then it can be open to challenge. Setting a precedent for helping a sweet old lady with her wheelie bin is hardly the same thing. In reality helping her out (or doing her a favour if you prefer this terminology) would hardly have opened the proverbial flood gates to thousands of people in the district demanding that we go into their houses, collect the bins, sweep the kitchen floor and clean the windows. And even if it did, so what? Deal with it when it happens and say no if people *are* actually taking advantage. But that approach would require a decision based on judgement rather than rules and may be too controversial. So no, in blind obedience to the rules, we make the wrong decision rather than running the risk of people finding out that rules in some cases are actually meant to be bent a little bit. Again if you stick to the rules, how can you possibly get it wrong?

Just as a footnote to this, the lady's assessment took about twelve weeks. During that time our bin lads had been informed of who she was and where she lived, they'd knocked on the door, introduced themselves, saw that she was not a malingerer (although they'd obviously not had the extensive social care training that was strictly necessary) and simply chose to use their own eyes and brains and, for the next few weeks, they walked the extra twenty yards down her garden and emptied her bin for her. This was all done without the knowledge of their manager until the assessment was completed and it became official. Well done boys, at least it proves that not all of us working at the council are Jobsworths.

Of course the whole example is one of simple bad management practice rather than anything else, but it does go to show that while the system advocates that the rules must be followed then managers and officers will use this as a way of avoiding decision making and continue to follow them, for better or for worse. There are plenty of council managers out there who act more responsibly but they have to spend time, effort and resources working around the system rather than the system working in the best interest of the electorate.

Most worrying of all is the fact that the vast majority of managers and officers do not oppose the ridiculous rules – they simply see it as their duty to ensure that they are enforced to the letter. So council staff are treated like fools and given no flexibility to actually make decisions. This means that where residents need an actual decision to be made they are fighting an uphill battle.

One-Size Fits No-one

"To Generalize is to be an Idiot; To Particularize is the Alone Distinction of Merit."
– William Blake

So why are all these rules in place anyway? Why has the element of decision making been so comprehensively removed? Why are we now in this bizarre position where this anonymous 'rules-based system' dominates everyone's life in the town hall?

It is hard to say how, why and when we arrived in this position. However, at the very top of this particular tree are our friends in Whitehall. Virtually everything that your town hall now does is not led by the local populous or the elected councillors. Instead, many of the ridiculous rules and regulations that are blindly implemented by the town hall officials are as a direct result of Whitehall chiefs having bright ideas about how to run things.

This is very much a top-down approach, which means that when a problem is highlighted to Whitehall the deskbound officials meet, discuss options, and come up with a series of measures that are then forced downwards to town halls across the country. While this top-down approach theoretically has its merits (consistency across the country, a common approach etc.) in practice it creates an extremely dependent and often unthinking culture within the average local authority.

This identikit approach to managing services requires the assessment and categorisation of virtually everything that councils deal with, from how well any particular child is performing in reading to how much care is required by an elderly resident, and from how clean a particular street is to how physically active people are being in their day to day lives. Everything, it seems, can now be reduced to a series of numbers, letters and priorities.

Yet, these are all complex problems that require skill, expertise and common-sense judgements. For many years experienced staff have been able to make decisions on how, for example, to care for old Mrs Dimpkins at No. 37. Does she need a home care worker, meals on wheels, adaptations to her home, support from relatives, or moving into sheltered accommodation? In reality, it is likely that some very specific combination of these is actually required for each particular person. And that is the key: every single person in the country is an individual and assigning them categories and numbers does little to genuinely improve services.

By making these assessments of people as if they are 'things' the people at the town hall have a much easier life though. Decision-making becomes, theoretically at least, much more simple because for every category that problems are put into there is an associated solution and action plan. Let's take Mrs Dimpkins as an ongoing example. At the first point the council becomes involved with her Mrs Dimpkins will have been assessed against dozens, if not hundreds, of different categories. This will have allowed someone sat in an office somewhere to type the information into a computer and to measure her against a national set of criteria. This will reveal that she is, let's say, a 2B at medium risk or a 3C at low risk. The numbers and names are arbitrary in any such assessment but they allow a 'tailored package' to be delivered to help the old dear. The process is easy for the paid official to manage because someone in category 2B gets solution 2B as defined by the appropriate guidance sheet.

Unfortunately these 'tailored packages' are rarely that. They are off-the-shelf solutions that help some and hinder others. Everyone who receives a service gets exactly what everyone else in their category gets. It's a little bit like horoscopes – if you are a Sagittarius those vague descriptions you see of the character traits of all Sagittarians are just that: vague descriptions. These descriptions and daily predictions are aimed at one in twelve of the population, so they are going to be right sometimes by the sheer weight of averages. In the same way, more often than not, the tailored package of support will be wide of the mark and the service offered won't be all of what is required.

Fans of this category approach to service delivery will simply try to refine the criteria, improve the assessment process and increase the number of possible categories. This, unfortunately, does not resolve the underlying issue that not everything can be solved by putting people into pigeonholes. The approach might help develop some understanding of problems and situations but when it is adhered to blindly, as it so often is by council officials, it simply creates inflexibility, an attitude of avoiding decision-making and ultimately offers a poor service for the electorate.

The main aim of this approach is to make sure that everyone up and down the country can expect the same level of service – like when you walk into a McDonald's 'restaurant'; whether you are in Swindon or Sunderland you know that a Big Mac will be exactly the same. But care for the elderly (and every other council service) is far more complex than assembling a burger and salad in a bun.

The guidance that councils receive does not remove the 'postcode lottery' that everyone seems so critical of. Instead they just replace one form of lottery with another. It becomes the random raffle of seeing which council will be most skilled at implementing the national directives rather than which ones can actually deliver the best services.

In fairness this approach has had one desired effect on councils up and down the country. The one size fits all has created a much more level playing field. Gone are the days where one council is fantastic at delivering national directives and the one next door is extremely poor. Now every single council (despite their different official ratings) is very 'much of a muchness', each offering services at slightly different levels of mediocrity, nothing more and nothing less. But then mediocrity is easy, nobody can have an issue with that. It seems that aiming for mediocrity is the answer; it's the minimum that's required by the electorate but easy to achieve. Everyone in the system is happy.

"It is no wonder that we all more or less delight in the mediocre, because it leaves us in peace: it gives us the comfortable feeling of intercourse with what is like ourselves."

– Johann Wolfgang Von Goethe

Such is the control exerted by the power mongers in Whitehall that every council in the country no longer truly manages its own work. Every system, project and structure must follow the one-size-fits-all checklist and categorisation approach and flexibility and common sense has become a thing of the best.

Some of you may be thinking that criticism of councils for this situation is a little unfair as they are being told what to do from above, in some cases with the threat of legal action, fines, or the withdrawal of funding. I see it differently. If councils truly felt that this was not the best way to deliver services they have the opportunity to lobby, argue and object, but they rarely – if ever – actually do. The combined might of just a handful of councils cannot be ignored and Whitehall's bluff could most certainly be called.

Despite all the internal spitting, whingeing and complaining, councils adopt the new guidance in the only way they know how – by senior managers selling it to staff and residents as a great idea that, at last, deals with the issue of 'xyz' and saying that they totally support the idea. Whether or not there is any real evidence that it works is pretty irrelevant to town hall executives. Once the idea has been sold to everyone involved, councils then proceed to develop their own individual systems to make the system work. That, at least, is the theory; in reality it simply allows the town hall to employ more people, develop new projects and drive more waste in to the system.

La Systeme

"Perfection is reached not when you have nothing else to add, but when you have nothing else to take away."

– Antoine de Saint-Exupéry

So what are these systems created by the apparatchiks at the town hall? First, I need to point out that these rules-based systems go far beyond the simple bureaucratic paper chases that pervade every town hall in the land. Pointless form filling is perhaps the thing that the average citizen is most familiar with, but behind this stockpile of paperwork is an even bigger and more cumbersome network of policies and procedures that ensure front line services continue to get less and less priority.

I shall start with an observation. During my all too brief period working in the private sector the main thing to avoid was 'double-handling'. This meant getting your raw materials in through the door, built up into the finished product and back out the door again as quickly as you can with as few people as possible being involved in the process in between. Mistakes in production must be avoided at all costs and when products go backwards in the production process (e.g. where the label on the tin of beans needs taking off and a new one putting on) costs escalate and heads roll. This is 'rework'. While town halls undoubtedly have some efficient systems the majority are far from it and rework seems to be the norm rather than the exception, with people and projects criss-crossing backwards and forwards almost randomly through the system rather than going in a fast, straight line through it.

This problem isn't because systems aren't running as they should; on the contrary, the systems run exactly as they are designed. It is the designs that are wrong. Far from avoiding steps in the process we insist on as many steps as possible to ensure that things are checked, inspected, audited and measured in every conceivable way.

When faced with a problem, rather than trying to find a solution the immediate response from senior and middle managers it is to build a brand new system of procedures (invariably based upon national legislation) that ensures not just that every 't' is crossed and every 'I' is dotted but that every word is underlined, written in italics and highlighted in the appropriate colour. The adage of 'why have one step in the process when a hundred will do' is what councils stand for in almost every case. So, instead of being able to get something done by a single officer in the interests of the public, we add a check, followed by a form, followed by a signature, followed by the same thing all over again.

And it is these myriad steps in the process that create all the problems. Steps take time. Steps mean mistakes are made. Steps mean that discretion is removed. Steps mean that things get lost. Steps mean that people can hide themselves in the system. Steps mean that individuals don't need to work anymore, they just push something from one step onto another without really knowing or caring what the next step is. But this flooding the system with additional steps just turns important and valuable processes that require thought and reasoning from the actors involved into a production line that Henry Ford would be proud of.

John Seddon (an expert in public sector systems) points out that, "Service organisations are not assembly lines; they are different kinds of systems. Working on people's activity will not solve the problem of errors, which are a product of the system. Managing people's activity will engage their ingenuity in surviving the system." The fact that small improvements can be made to the system through 'business process reengineering' or whatever fad is in fashion simply shows that each step can be improved (slightly) but that on the whole things have got so convoluted and bulky that to strip out the entire system root and branch is something that no one would be able to comprehend.

But I have to admit that a little part of me sort of enjoys working within '*la systeme*'. It allows me to be a seen as a 'maverick', which makes me feel like the Dirty Harry of our town hall. It's a sad little world I live in admittedly but being a maverick in the town hall is easy. You don't need to intimidate people or leap through plate glass windows. No, it's much easier. Just forget to fill in the appropriate form to change a budget heading code and you are seen by the operators of the system as reckless as well as being accused of playing fast and loose with protocol. You really have to see it to believe how seriously some people take these very unimportant steps.

"Men are moved by two levers only: fear and self-interest."

– Napoleon Bonaparte

Napoleon's quote above is a kind of one line version of what the boffins call 'public choice theory'. The theory suggests that human beings are primarily motivated not by kindness or altruism but rather by the desire to maximise their own self-interest. When applied to your average town hall this means that council managers are likely to be motivated only with achieving a pay rise for themselves and to have as big a department under their control as possible. While there are undoubtedly plenty of managers for whom this is true the theory leaves little room to acknowledge the existence of those who are kind and self-motivated who just want to run effective services.

Whatever the strengths and weaknesses of this theory (and there are many of both explored far more fully elsewhere) one thing is certainly true. To try and avoid any possibility of self-interest councils have put into place some of the most bulky and cumbersome procedures known to man.

Many of these procedures and systems are financially based, developed in the first instance to stop shady council officials taking backhanders from fly-by-night companies, and in the second instance by monitoring every single penny spent to show how efficient council services are.

I have one major observation to make on the first of these points. This is that during my time in local government I have encountered only two people who could be described as 'iffy'. These individuals, who shall for obvious reasons remain nameless, were 'dodgy' through and through. However, the systems that were put in place did not stop them from taking backhanders, which they pocketed on a regular basis. Only good management and strong leaders can do that. I've been offered bribes myself and they have been presented in such a way that that, had I been inclined to accept them, absolutely no-one within the authority would have been any the wiser.

Putting procedural controls in place does not stop the genuine criminals; it only makes it harder for everyone else. Suppliers and staff spend more time and effort thinking their way around and through systems just to get things done rather than actually doing something useful.

The principle of monitoring every single penny is a

tougher one to critique. But the necessity to justify everything, combined with the top-down categorisation and checklist approach, has led every local authority to have systems that are so wasteful that my old Mum's adage of 'penny-wise, pound foolish' has found the perfect home. The scrutiny that should take place about where the money actually goes is lax to say the least.

Let me give an example. Virtually every service in your town hall will have its own administration/finance team that monitors every invoice and receipt that comes across its desk. Invariably there is also the corporate finance team who monitor the budgets of the council as a whole.

All this is fine (I guess) and ultimately it means that every penny is accounted for; there is a paper trail for the auditors (yet another council team) to follow when needed. In short, every pencil, bin wagon and tonne of tarmac can be traced, checked and ticked off. Fantastic... the same is true of every penny given to officers in wages. Everything is there in black and white. However, there is something fundamental that most councils seem to miss. Those people carrying out the audits and checks do not assess whether the money has been well spent on the right things, but merely account for money being spent on what it said it has been spent on. This is a very subtle but very important distinction.

When operating your household budget you are not interested in whether or not the invoice from your plumber is on the correctly headed paper, and shows the correct reference number and date. No. You are interested in whether the work carried out is to a good standard, whether it is good value for money and, indeed, whether the work needed to be done in the first place. For big organisations the right paperwork is understandably important but for councils the paperwork has become the end rather than part of the means. People have forgotten in this huge council machine that value for money and spending money on the right things are what's important.

So, while the pennies that go out of the front door are getting looked after in excruciating detail, millions of pounds are spent going out of the back door on unnecessary people and systems. However, this seems to be OK with the powers that be because every penny can be explained so everything in the garden *must* be rosy.

Sorry to lapse into management speak here but what councils are incredibly talented at is missing the 'bigger picture'. By this I mean that they have become increasingly effective at looking after the minutiae. Systems and processes are developed in complete isolation from each other with little or no thought to their impact on the wider community, other council services or colleagues in other public services. Worse still, every council makes claims about how it is making big strategic decisions, working in partnerships, and taking the helicopter view etc., but in reality I have yet to work for one authority that really, honestly and truly understands what it is doing. And for a collection of organisations that manage billions of pounds worth of your money that is very worrying indeed.

Activity without Achievement:
The role of bureaucracy and entrepreneurism

"Are South Derbyshire really that bad?"
"Yes, they won't send in their blue forms."
"I really don't see how life can go on in Derbyshire!"
– Yes Minister

Bureaucracy in town halls is everyone's favourite topic to poke fun at so I will endeavour to maintain a little bit of dignity here and avoid simply laughing at the pencil pushing and form filling that I am sure every reader can reel off a dozen examples of. Bureaucracy is often seen as something rather laughable and wasteful but not as a genuinely harmful influence. Personally, I see it a little more seriously than this.

My first observation to make about bureaucracy in the council is from an example that appears in Mark Moore's book, *Creating Public Value*. In considering the lack of entrepreneurism in the public sector Moore gives the example of a librarian in the USA. This librarian noticed that her building was being frequented by lots of children, the 'latch-key kids', who used the library as somewhere warm and friendly they could go to after school. Rather than kicking the kids out (because they might cause problems) the librarian decided to embrace the idea of getting more children into the library. She looked at setting up a kids club that allowed these children (and lots of others) to use the library as a stop off, and to encourage a greater involvement in books and reading.

What a great example of how things should run. When reading this story my thoughts turned to how this would be managed by my own local authority. First, the librarian in question would be disciplined for overstepping her role; no doubt her managers would question her ability to run a library and she would be made to feel guilty for having a positive idea.

Even if her department managers didn't take this approach and decided that the idea was a good one and that they wanted to keep it going that is the point at which the bureaucratic system would rumble into action. This would mean that everyone working in the library from the librarians to the cleaners would need to have police criminal record checks carried out; changes to the building would need to be done to ensure it was secure for children's activities to run; national standards would need to be met for staffing levels, training and the number of children allowed in the building; consent forms would need signing by all the parents; numerous risk assessments would need carrying out and, finally, a monitoring programme would need to be created to see how effective the whole thing is at addressing inequality.

And it is this requirement for red tape at every possible step that creates so many frustrations and means that services delivered are a long way short of what they could be. Local authority managers design projects and services that are so complicated that they have to provide training courses and guidance notes to demystify them, and to use support offices to provide further advice.

But this is how the system has been designed. It is far easier for everyone involved to work with something that has the step-by-step process mapped out and where the end result is actually unimportant as long as the process has been followed. As I am regularly told by my managers, following the procedures is very, very important. It is far more important than actually providing a good service anyway. Besides, what could be better than, at the end of the year, announcing with due pride that although we are unable to give decent services to members of the public we have managed to 'process' more than a thousand DFG001/A forms. I'm sure everyone involved is suitably proud.

"All of us have a natural tendency towards bureaucracy. It would have been much easier to chalk up on the cave wall the number of woolly mammoths trapped than actually to go out and trap woolly mammoths. Likewise, nowadays, it is much easier to sit behind a desk and draw graphs about problems than it is to actually get off your backside and sort out the problems."

– PC David Copperfield

And so town officials are in the position where they no

longer work for the local electorate but rather work to feed the bureaucratic machine. This is where the real danger lies, and this is where I enter some very shaky ground. But, like I say, I enjoy being a maverick.

The controversial case of the death of Baby Peter in Haringey hit the headlines and had a huge impact. Commentators, with the usual knee-jerk reaction, started a witch hunt for the guilty individuals in the social services team (or Children's Services, as it is now known). Understandably the anger aimed at those involved was palpable, but very few people will have realised that those people who were involved from the local authority and other public agencies were not necessarily the only ones to blame.

Without wishing to defend the actions of those involved, as mistakes were clearly made, I want to point out that the bureaucratic system that has been developed in the area of child protection is also partly to blame. But, criticising the paperwork doesn't sell papers or satisfy the public desire to hang someone for what happened. Indeed, the public outcry was such that the social workers involved were more reviled than the sickening individuals who beat, tortured and murdered a defenceless baby. The required paperwork in Haringey and every other local authority up and down the country means that the role of social workers is no longer to protect children but to demonstrate that they are protecting children. The distinction between the two must be understood.

To demonstrate you are protecting children means that you need to fill in endless computerised forms, targets need to be hit to ensure these forms are checked and processed, and budgets need to be met. This means that rather than concentrating on the job in hand, which is to inspect and investigate cases, time is spent on the periphery and decision-making rests not with the front line workers but with people in the back office who make decisions based on budgets and paperwork. In the name of 'making sure that individuals don't make mistakes', bureaucracy has removed any ability to make judgement calls.

Bureaucracy, then, has paradoxically increased the chances of mistakes being made because people are concentrating on things that aren't actually important. This means they take the eye off the ball and people and problems 'fall between the gaps' in the system. When mistakes do happen, reviews then take place that simply state that we need more joined up working, and yet another step is put into the system to help bolster things. But the system contains humans and human beings make mistakes; no bureaucratic system in the world will ever remove that and, indeed, badly designed processes simply make things worse.

Fundamentally, town halls have become a product of years and years of bureaucracy that has simply built upwards and outwards, as new forms and procedures are added. While this is downright wasteful because of the need for extra resources to keep the machine running, the hidden costs are much, much greater.

While the headlines will always be grabbed when multi-million pound IT systems crash and burn or where investigation has shown that thousands are spent every day by town halls on stationery, printing or support staff, in reality we should always look behind the headlines to see what impact bureaucracy has on the services that millions of us depend on every day. I doubt anyone will ever be able to fully grasp and quantify the real cost of bureaucracy but I hope that people will start to see that it goes way beyond the simple cost of a person's wage added to the cost of the paper and ink they use.

Officer Ability

"The purpose of bureaucracy is to compensate for incompetence and a lack of discipline – a problem that largely goes away if you have the right people in the first place. Most [organisations] build their bureaucratic rules to manage the small percentage of wrong people in the organisation, which in turn drives the right people away, which in turn increases the percentage of wrong people in the organisation, which increases the need for more bureaucracy to compensate for incompetence and lack of discipline and so on and so forth."

– Jim Collins

As an avid (sad) reader of various internet discussion forums I notice that whenever a newspaper features an article relating to local authority ineptitude or waste there is almost immediately a deluge of posts that criticise the ability of anyone who works in a town hall. The belief is that those that can, do. Those that can't, teach. Public opinion today should perhaps add that those that can't teach join local government.

Were you to take a walk round your own town hall I suspect there would be little to convince you that this is not the case. In the various authorities I have worked in I have met very few individuals I would describe as genuinely inspirational or dynamic. That is not to say that I haven't worked with some intelligent and gifted people who work very hard. However, the overall culture of all my authorities has been one whereby excellence is not rewarded effectively and where ineptitude is hidden. This creates a level playing field where those few really good people are dragged down to match the standards of the poorest ones. Of course every organisation in the world, public or private, has a mixture of abilities, but local authorities have institutionalised mediocrity and readily accept lower levels of ability amongst its workers than they have any right to.

To be inept and awful at your job used to be something that would make you fearful for your job. Certainly in the private sector this would be the case. In the town hall, however, it would take something really special for a useless officer to actually get the chop. Indeed, as shown in the examples I have given previously, even illegal activities do not guarantee the sack. My colleagues joke that assaulting our chief executive would only result in a wrist- slapping and an anger management course.

The second reason for the culture of mediocrity is the lack of any challenges in the work people do in local authorities. Not making decisions is now the mantra for everyone sat behind their cosy desks in councils and who wouldn't take advantage of this given the opportunity. Promotion comes not from an excellent record of achievement but from staying out of trouble, from not sticking your head above the parapet and generally not being noticed. This means that the culture is one of sitting back and waiting for things to happen. Those people who do a hundred things a day are looked on with suspicion. After all, doing a hundred things means that you are likely to get criticised for at least one or two of them. If you only do one thing a day, and concentrate really hard on making sure no one notices, that becomes the way to succeed at the council. This is the way in which average people receive plaudits for adequate results. Lower ability individuals get plaudits for their consistency and for never having made a mistake.

Another reason for officers not performing to high standards is something that occurred to me after seeing a quotation from Frederick Herzberg. He suggested that, "If you want people to do a good job, give them a good job to do." Standards are fundamentally so low because people are given such low level, menial jobs to do. People are not empowered to perform well when, instead of having the authority to do something useful, they are given nothing more interesting than the responsibility of filling in a form. The whole thing essentially becomes a vicious cycle – jobs get more and more pointless, the standard of people doing the job gets lower and lower, and so on and so forth, ad infinitum. In some cases staff that have their jobs deskilled to such an extent that they have to lower their own efforts and input.

"The curriculum for most professional exams [within local government] emphasised a need to acquire a meticulous grasp of facts and legal procedures rather than any ability to think innovatively. The emphasis on competence rather than understanding and innovative capacity within NVQ qualifications thus exerts a considerable attraction for more pedestrian local authorities."

– J A Chandler

Councils, by their very structure, are the best environment for those who love detail, that enjoy structure, hierarchy and documentation. While I wouldn't be dismissive enough to just say that organisations do not need people like this I would question whether quite so many are needed in councils. Rarely do I walk into departments in my town hall without coming out wondering whether the electorate want to rely on people who feel they are doing a good job provided they are filling out forms and spreadsheets and who enjoy not having to think for themselves. Ultimately though, for all the reasons I have given above, council staff who may have the potential to be a lot better rarely actually push the boundaries or go the extra mile. For too long council workers have been in far too privileged a position and, as a result, have grown flabby and lazy. It's not that they are inactive and don't work hard and have intelligence. No, rather it is that some are working hard but on the wrong things and that the skills people do have are not fully utilised. It has also become very easy to remain hidden and any organisation that can mask ineptitude in this way becomes quite an attraction to lazy workers.

It is this attitude that is perhaps most abhorrent to me. Your town hall should be full of the most enthusiastic and committed individuals – people who are passionate about making a difference; people who will bust a gut to make the world even just a slightly better place. Sadly, it just isn't. Most of the departments are a metaphorical graveyard inhabited by people who perhaps once had passion and desire but now behave like suet puddings.

A Way Forward

"Mr Jones' results are terrible and they always have been. Thanks to the teachers unions, however, he will never be sacked; he will simply go on being bad and not teaching maths until he retires."

– Frank Chalk

Only by removing some of the opportunities for milking the system will councils become a more proactive place to work. Removing just some of the fringe benefits can only be a step in the right direction. This doesn't mean the wholesale removal of everyone's terms and conditions, it means stripping out some of the more ridiculous opportunities people have to take the Mickey.

More fundamentally, leaders need to take the brave step of overhauling virtually all the systems and procedures that operate in town halls. This most certainly does not mean recruiting external consultants to come in and reshape all the processes to make them slicker through the latest new approach; whether that is six-sigma, business process reengineering, or whatever.

Instead, leaders have to be confident in the good staff who still remain in town halls. They need to stop being fearful of doing things, of taking decisions and of making mistakes. They need to accept that the busier they get and the more things that they actually do then the more mistakes will be made but that in the long term the council will achieve far, far more and, in addition, councils will receive more respect from the residents that they are there to serve.

Stripping out the bureaucracy can only be achieved once the leaders in the town hall truly understand the systems that they look after. This does not mean mapping the processes and creating lists of steps in the system to see which ones can be cut out. It means understanding the interdependency of every department in the council. Some good might come from understanding the butterfly effect; this is the notion that if a butterfly flaps its wings in America, it causes a hurricane in China. The fact that how roads are designed and built has an impact on how they cleaned and maintained; that creating a new checklist and assessment in one arena creates difficulties for those delivering services in another.

The stripping out of the bureaucracy means that the emphasis will start to shift from a rules-based system to a customer-care based system, such that council employees have the information and authority to make the best decision for people who need our assistance. It will encourage people to join the public sector for more public-spirited reasons as opposed to selfish ones. It will help to remove the career public servant and instead bring some entrepreneurial spirit that will allow people to take chances and to try things that improve their area.

Anyone who can truly understand all the interdependency and also has the ability to change the emphasis of local authorities onto people rather than rules is a far better person than I. This means fundamentally doing away with a vast number of systems. Not all of them, of course – large organisations need to manage the practicalities of paying invoices, managing maintenance etc. – but for too long we have tweaked around the edges and not managed to change a single thing. Systems need ripping out and starting from the ground up. Difficult though it will be, it is possible to do this, the willingness just needs to be there.

5. "It's Like Wetting Yourself in a Dark Blue Suit"

It's Like What?

"Partnership working is a bit like wetting yourself in a dark blue suit. It gives you a nice, warm feeling for a while, but ultimately nobody really notices – or cares."

The above is something I heard at a seminar I went to some years ago (yes, sorry – it was at your expense) where a very senior police officer was talking about the practicalities of 'partnership working'. I found the reference amusing at the time as he went on to explain how wrong this vision of partnership really was when compared with the proper approach. I have long since forgotten the rest of his speech, which probably says more about my attitude to partnerships than the quality of Officer Dibble's speech.

So, for the uninitiated, you might be asking what partnership working is. On one website it states that partnership working:

"…is at the heart of the agenda for improving outcomes and making local services cost effective. The Audit Commission describes a partnership as a joint-working arrangement where the partners:

- Are otherwise independent bodies

- Agree to cooperate to achieve a common goal

- Create a new organisational structure or process to achieve this goal, separate from their own organisations

- Plan and implement a jointly agreed programme, often with joint staff or resources

- Share relevant information

- Pool risks and rewards.

Partnerships and integrated working require a culture of shared ownership and common working arrangements across organisational and professional boundaries."

An example might be a Safer Neighbourhoods Partnership where the police, the fire brigade, council civil enforcement officers, housing agencies, neighbourhood watch and the youth offending teams get together to discuss and address crime and anti-social behaviour problems.

These principles are similar across the board – local authority officers work together with a variety of other organisations, from the NHS to local community groups, quangos and/or statutory agencies in order to achieve something greater than the sum of their parts.

All sounds fantastic doesn't it? And indeed it would be if it were really like that. Unfortunately, as you'll see, practice is, as ever, somewhat different from the theory.

Partnerships have always existed in one format or another. Originally it was fairly informal; the local beat bobby might ring his contact in the local council to see if anything could be done about the vandalism in the local park. Or vice-versa. Now, in this brave new world, this informal arrangement has become a formal partnership with all the associated costs, headaches and problems. Partnerships have become more 'strategic'; senior officers sign agreements to work together, partnerships have to be evidenced, meetings held, reams of documents produced and managers come in to make working together more problematic – sorry, I mean more straightforward.

So rather than delivering the Audit Commission's 'cost effective services' they become unwieldy, time-wasting bureaucracies.

It Just Doesn't Quite Work Like That

"A committee is a thing that takes a week to do what one good man can do in an hour."

– Anon

In order for a partnership to be successful everyone around the table must have a common purpose for sitting there. This is a key problem with many partnerships from the outset. Put simply, the police do not have the same priorities as the fire brigade, who in turn do not have the same priorities as housing agencies. And while people involved in the partnership might agree on the need to do things, when it comes to actually moving resources around to hit these shared priorities things start to fall down.

The intention is that partnerships bring organisations

together over specific issues that are not necessarily the responsibility of one organisation. Take childhood obesity, for example. Many local councils are part of partnerships with the local NHS, as well as schools, sports clubs, and voluntary organisations to help deliver a series of actions which can influence the diet and exercise levels of young people in a specific area. Again it all sounds good in principle but the problem is that the people sitting round the table have their own organisational priorities, things that they have to be doing no matter what else is happening in the world.

Some partnerships have actually been set up on fundamentally unsound principles. One example that I see on a regular basis are Neighbourhood Action Teams (NATs). These are set up in many areas to bring together those people who have an impact on low level crime and anti-social behaviour in the local neighbourhood (often an electoral ward area – so our particular authority has fourteen NATs). Each NAT has representation from local ward councillors, police beat officers/local sergeants, youth services, neighbourhood services (street cleaners et al), neighbourhood watch coordinators and often local schools and parish or town councils.

That's a lot of people sat around a lot of tables. Nothing is wrong with that in principle, but on every occasion I have attended these partnership meetings they have been an opportunity for people to report things like graffiti on a garage wall, to complain about dog mess on the pavement outside their house or to report children in the park causing an annoyance. These are things that are naturally important to individual people but there are other channels for these complaints, i.e. directly to the right service in the council or the police.

Partnerships are meant to tackle those issues that cannot be addressed by individuals but they end up merely talking about the things that should have been sorted out very easily previously, and becomes a way of escalating a very basic problem that only really needs a conversation between two people (the beat copper and the park warden) into something bigger and more problematic. In short, the council have helped to set up a partnership to resolve a problem that they have created in the first place. In other words they have managed to remove power from individuals and departments, realised that nothing is really getting done as a result and so created partnerships to solve the 'problem'. These partnerships have little genuine power to address, say, anti-social behaviour, short of hard-hitting actions like... er... erm... er... leaflet drops or promotional market stalls. These are things that must scare all the local villains! In short, the partnership can agree actions all day long, but as an entity it means nothing. These actions are simply things that can and should be done as individual departments, like cleaning off some graffiti on a garage wall. The whole is just about equal to the sum of its parts – no value is added.

NATs don't stop there. Once issues have been raised at the neighbourhood level, with the ten or twelve people at those meetings, things that aren't sorted at that stage can be reported up to another level of partnership. NATs are overseen by AATs (Area Action Teams). AATs are made up of representatives from perhaps three or four NATs who come together with more 'strategic' officers from the council and other organisations to address the bigger issues – whatever they are. The intention is that the managers who allocate resources and set priorities will listen to this group more than they would do to individual complaints or issues. But shouldn't managers be listening anyway? Some think that the AATs have the power to really 'do' something, but unfortunately they still do very little; they just do it at a higher level with higher paid people sat round the table.

The good news is that the issues that haven't been

sorted out through the NATs or the AATs have yet another layer where they can be heard. The SNATs are the final layer of partnership that should have the capability of resolving any issue that comes their way, from global warming to the world financial crisis. The trouble is that the people in this group are the managers of the people in the other groups and as a rule they prefer to give non-committal answers, to delay making decisions and to resort to political spin. But at least residents can rest assured that their particular issues have been raised at the highest level, even if it has taken six months to go through the full cycle of meetings and agendas. In a perfect world, of course, the resident might be able to get his or her issue addressed by the right people on the front line or to speak directly to the head person if things aren't sorted out. But that would be far too easy and would mean that lots of people in the system would become surplus to requirements.

(Not) getting things done!

"Meetings are indispensable when you don't want to do anything."

– J K Galbraith

My main problem with the partnership approach is not the principles that underlie it (sharing resources and knowledge, combining forces etc.) but the practical application of it. While many partnerships herald their achievements (which, at times, can be impressive) at every available opportunity, one has to sit back for a moment and think, OK, this work has been done but is a formal partnership approach the only, or indeed the best way, of actually achieving something. As in the example above (NATs, AATs, SNATs), partnerships seem to be increasing in number, yet the work that needs to be completed seems not to increase at all. In my opinion, if crime levels are an issue, then the police should lead, and if they need something to be done by the council they should ask them to do it. The informal partnerships of the past, where if the police needed some areas cleaning up of graffiti etc. they just spoke to their contact at the Council, were a much more efficient way of getting a job done. Does it really need to go through a formal partnership meeting?

Even the simplest of tasks, it seems, are subject to partnerships or at the very least a requirement to get all the 'key stakeholders' around the table to agree the way forward. Our town hall officials are now so brainwashed by the partnership solution that it seems to be applied to virtually everything. Partnerships are set up on a daily basis not just between organisations but also within the council itself; task groups are set up between various services to deal with one thing or another, steering groups are created to address other problems. It all comes down to the same thing – people sat around a table discussing things rather than the right people actually just getting the things done. But, anyone who concentrates on just getting their own job done is accused of being blinkered, not networking, operating in isolation or 'having their own agenda'.

Let me give an example of how things seem to operate. It's a facetious example, but then again it's meant to be.

Real Life:

Problem:

- The grass is getting too long

Action:

- Get the lawnmower out and cut the grass

Timescale:

- Before lunchtime this Saturday

In Partnership:

Problem:

- The grass is getting too long

Organisations to include:

- Biodiversity Team – to monitor the impact on the local wildlife

- Health and Safety Team – to ensure that all the necessary risk assessments are complete for the use of the lawnmower and associated activities

- Local Resident Groups/Neighbourhood Watch – to ensure that all local people are aware of the plans to cut the grass

- Environmental Health Team – to make sure any noise created by the lawnmower does not contravene acceptable noise levels

- Commissioning Team – to investigate the possibility of commissioning out any grass cutting works to a third party organisation

- Audit and Standards Team – to monitor the quality of the grass cutting to ensure appropriate standards are met

- Voluntary Community Sector organisations – to potentially bid to carry out the necessary grass cutting operations

- Police – is the lawnmower secured effectively when not in use? Does using the lawnmower create any anti-social behaviour problems?

- Unions – to ensure that the plan to cut the grass does not contravene any employment agreements

- Public Health – to see if mowing the lawn can be promoted more widely as a healthy activity to combat obesity

- Grounds Maintenance Unit – to actually carry out any necessary work

Actions:

- Invite representatives from all the organisations to attend an initial meeting to discuss the way forward

- Agree a draft action plan

- Circulate the action plan to everyone and await amendments

- Reconvene meeting to finalise and approve the action plan, carrying out any necessary consultation with local residents

- Designate actions to the appropriate partners involved

- Carry out necessary actions (hopefully)

- Reconvene meeting to monitor and evaluate success (or otherwise) of cutting the grass

- Issue press releases throughout the period of the action plan to ensure the public are aware of the good work being carried out and to present them with the opportunity to be part of the consultation process

Timescale:

- About three months

The serious message is that if you look hard enough everyone is a 'stakeholder' in everything. To try and involve organisations in services is not in itself a bad thing but there is a scale to consider here. Now if cutting the grass can be made so complicated, imagine the conversations that take place when trying to address something a bit tougher, like anti-social behaviour. In fairness all bureaucracies (private and public sector) operate in this long-handed way. However, partnerships take it to a whole new level simply in terms of the numbers involved and because of the extremely diverse agendas at the table and the resulting pressures and disagreements that result.

One partnership meeting I was involved in a few years ago talked at length about the removal of some old garage blocks on a council estate in one of our larger towns. I would guess around twenty people were sat round the table chomping on biscuits and banging the world to rights. The majority of these people managed their own budget (however large or small) and were all intelligent and educated people of some seniority in their respective organisations or services.

The meeting started with everyone watching a specially commissioned ten-minute DVD. The film had been put together over the previous two or three weeks and consisted of 'partnership staff' interviewing local residents and partnership agencies about their thoughts on the garages, what should happen to them and the problems they were encountering. The DVD and discussions amongst the group showed a strong consensus: the garages were frequently being set alight, were no longer used to store cars by residents, suffered regular vandalism and created a hot spot for crime. Decision made then, everyone chips in some of their budget to get them knocked down, the area is made safe and work is carried out to create a community area with car parking and landscaping... easy!

If only. Everyone at the meeting, as well as the residents in the area, agreed that the garages needed to be knocked down, but the partnership approach meant that further research was needed. A survey was requested to undertake an options appraisal and this was to be reported on to the partnership within six months.

I sat in the meeting pleading the case for a bit of sanity – for everyone involved (police, fire brigade, housing association and council) to contribute some of their own budgets to get the necessary work carried out. The police would have fewer call outs, the fire brigade would have fewer fires to put out, the housing association and council would have less vandalism to repair and the residents would still have somewhere to park their cars without the associated problems that the garages brought. Surely everyone would be a winner.

But no one around the table felt able to chip in a few quid from their budgets (after all, their budgets need protecting at all costs, and as far as they were concerned doing something for the greater good could wait, if it meant they got to keep hold of every last penny). They didn't want to make this kind of earth-shattering decision (even as part of the wider group) and I can only surmise that they thought that as long as the problem was 'being looked at' then they were sort of solving the problem.

The example is a small and minor one but this attitude is reflected across many of the partnerships I have worked with. Sometimes things just need to be done and a partnership only adds mass to the system. Dismissing partnerships in this way is not the same as dismissing involvement, but rather encourages people to look at the most effective way to get services delivered rather than resorting to partnership working as an opportunity to tick a box.

I have been to dozens of partnership meetings and have yet to be impressed by what goes on at them. There are few enough inspirational people working at the town hall (though there are some) but these meetings seem to bring together everything that's wrong with staff who work for authorities. I have invariably been one of the most junior staff at these meetings (by a clear fifteen or twenty thousand pounds a year in most cases) and the sheer lack of progress is disgusting. When it comes to discussing actually carrying out some work it is, invariably, the least senior staff at the meetings that discuss things and agree actions. The senior staff seem to have forgotten the purpose of their work and the principle of 'doing something', and so they will just sit in silence whilst others try (and that's the key word) to get something positive out of the partnership.

The Supporting Infrastructure

"To get something done a committee should consist of no more than three people, two of whom are absent."

– Robert Copeland

Aside from the lack of real progress made by partnerships the additional cottage industry that has grown up around servicing them is another major concern. As we will see later, work in local authorities cannot be completed without an accompanying 'strategy' and almost every piece of work carried out by town officials also needs the validity that only partnership support can bring. Without having this support from the appropriate group of people sat round a meeting room table with their coffee and croissants, no work is considered worthwhile for its own ends.

Partnerships tend to be attended by back room managers or development workers and not by front line workers. This means that meetings take place often for their own sake i.e. to satisfy the 'professional meeting attenders' who go. It is in their best interest, then, to ensure the meetings continue otherwise they'd have nothing to fill their days. Every private company has people like this but councils seem to have turned it into an art form.

In order to service and support themselves a large number of partnerships across the country have their own extra staff and resources. At the most basic level this means someone to, say, take the minutes of meetings, book venues etc. This could be someone already in existence within the authority who is given extra work (and sometimes extra hours) to do the job but might equally be someone recruited specifically for the job.

This is only the tip of the iceberg, however. Many more partnerships take on a whole realm of support staff in order to further justify their existence. They meet on a not infrequent basis to discuss various issues; often employing a manager and even a small team of administrative staff to do their bidding. Their bidding is, more likely than not, to ask for more information or to invite people along to the next meeting rather than to actually carry out something clear and tangible for the benefit of the populous.

The rationale behind recruiting staff is fairly self-serving; the thinking is that if a 'partnership' has staff then it's a real thing that can be pointed to and used as best practice. A partnership without staff (or least without some additional resource) could be seen by others as nothing more than a talking shop (heaven forbid) but if your partnership has people employed to deliver things then others will look on with envy and appreciate that your partnership is really delivering something.

So we are left in a strange position where each council employs not just people to deliver your frontline services, not just people to then manage these services, not just all the backroom staff to support these services and not just all the other 'non-services' we have already seen but also a new breed of 'partnership' staff who are there to do little more than share information, talk amongst themselves and be seen to address the big issues.

Partnership Development

"People who enjoy meetings should not be in charge of anything."

– Thomas Sowell

So, one of the most worrying things about partnerships is the sheer number of them that are out there and they seem to reproduce at an alarming rate. From simply looking at just a few council websites the emphasis that is placed on developing partnerships is clear. One of the first websites I looked at proudly promoted its very own partnership development unit. That is people who are solely employed, not to actually make any improvements to their local area, but to get people sat round a table to chat about things. Whether or not things actually improved as a result of these chats seemed unimportant; rather it was important enough just to get a tick in the box to demonstrate that the partnership had been set up. Even those councils that do not have a dedicated team to develop partnerships will have officers who are located in various services whose sole aim is to bring people together in this way.

Having said this, judging by the information that's out there, those councils that do have a partnership development unit should be extremely proud of their achievements. Indeed, the staff involved in those units should be on some kind of performance related pay; what they have achieved is mind blowing. The second local authority website I looked at very kindly listed all their partnerships in alphabetical order; there were 167 in total!

Remember this isn't a list of organisations or council services, this is a list of 'partnerships' where people from about half a dozen organisations get together to address something and nothing in particular. I won't embarrass the local authority in question by naming them but suffice to say that they were not unusual and were not one of the larger authorities in the country. Some of the more amusing and disconcerting partnerships include:

Culture Theme Group

Multi Area Agreement Group

CAA Strategic Lead Officers Group

Consultants Partnerships

Design and Heritage Forum

Climate Change Coalition

Archaeological Committee

Hard to Reach and Travellers Forum

Event Management Group

Bus Quality Partnership

Town Twinning Partnership

Joint Archives Advisory Board

Community Planning Partnership

Section 75 Partnership (don't ask, I don't know either!)

While not every partnership is replicated in every local authority many are. If every council in the country is involved in say a hundred local partnerships (and this is a conservative estimate) there must be more than forty or fifty thousand partnership meetings taking place on a monthly or quarterly basis up and down the country. There may be some valuable work going on but the scale of bureaucracy is mind boggling.

Admittedly, not all the partnerships above are huge, cumbersome, resource intensive leviathans but they *all* involve public servants at the town hall spending time and effort attending meetings and discussing actions, approaches and plans to deliver questionable improvements, Compare this to employing someone just to get the job done. The spin-doctors would have you believe that these partnerships are greater than the sum of their parts. In my experience they simply give more people the opportunity to sit around and procrastinate and to put lots of things in the 'too hard to deal with' column. But at least they get agreement on that point so everything is tickety-boo.

One of the best scams to be pulled by councils on a regular basis is the 'regional partnership'; these mirror the local partnerships with one key difference. They are an even bigger waste. These regional partnerships mean that council officers from five, ten or even twenty town halls get to meet up on a regular basis to 'network and share best practice'. Naturally, if there is something that can be learnt from a neighbouring authority then I am all in favour of using their idea. Of course this can't simply involve a telephone conversation between two people. It involves seminars, conferences, meetings, forums, action plans, tea and sympathy. They cover almost all areas of council work too, from highways to leisure centres and from urban planning to education. Everyone gets the chance to go to events and avoid doing work for the local electorate.

(Why not check out your own local council's website to see some of your own more amusing partnerships. Some of them might even be looking for new volunteers from the local community so please stick your name down – it will be a real eye opener.)

Confrontation and Blame

"You can accomplish anything in life providing you do not mind who gets the credit."

– Harry S Truman

Working at the town hall always seems to provide numerous examples of the 'Law of Unintended Consequences'. In short, we can decide to take a particular action without a sense of what the consequences might be. These consequences are not actually intended, and in most cases they are not even considered. Partnerships often have their own unintended consequence: conflict.

In many arenas a bit of 'clear the air' conflict is a good thing. On the very rare occasions that my wife and I fall out, a bit of shouting and hollering can often make us both feel better. Not at the time, perhaps, but certainly in the long run once the broken dishes have been picked up. In partnerships the conflict that is created is not simply about personality clashes between certain individuals. It is often institutionalised and systemic and is far more harmful as a result.

SORRY, IT'S NOT MY DEPARTMENT

In the private sector the relationship between different companies is fairly clear. Companies in competition with each other may operate with a mutual or begrudging respect, but very rarely work together unless it is to meet up at a national trade event to compare notes and get drunk together or, for the conspiracy theorist amongst you, to have clandestine meetings to fix prices and share out the big juicy contracts amongst themselves.

Similarly the supply chain relationships are also quite clear despite the recent move towards stronger and closer working relationships between customers and suppliers. In short, companies want to get their materials and equipment as cheaply as possible from their suppliers and to charge as much as possible to their end customers. The way this is done might be very complicated, but the principle is very simple and any conflict is purely down to different companies not wanting their profit margins to be squeezed too tightly.

Conflict between different bodies in partnerships is far more complicated than this. At the most basic level sometimes the conflict created is purely down to personal grudges and history (again you get this with any group of people sat round a table) but the system of partnerships is set up in such a way as to create conflict.

An example of this comes from the way that national funding is distributed to local councils and some of the work they carry out. Rather than the national government simply handing money over to local authorities (although it is kind of understandable why they don't) they insist that councils demonstrate (to the Nth degree) how they work in partnership with various organisations first. Again, fine in principle but in practice this creates difficulties.

While organisations are encouraged to work together in partnerships for the greater good and to allow them to get their hands on the cash this is only half the story. For the rest of the time these same organisations are encouraged to make applications for other pots of funding in competition with the same people they are also expected to work together with. This is particularly true of neighbouring local authorities who work in combination with each other on regional funding applications but who are then in competition with each other to receive government regeneration funds. For example, only twenty local authorities throughout the country might be selected to receive a certain stream of funding. Funding can come from national government, the EU, regional bodies, and grant making organisations like the BIG Lottery. The principles remain the same, though: work in partnerships to get our money, but at the same time you will be competing with other organisations who last week you were working alongside.

Really it's like asking two groups to work together in one breath and saying, "Play nicely together and you'll get some money," and then the next day throwing some cash into the middle of the room and making the self-same groups compete by bidding for it. This system is hardly conducive to long-lasting trust and respect; rather, it creates double standards and back biting. The question you might ask yourself is, "Would two competing private businesses build a relationship in this way?"

A second reason for conflict is the way that voluntary (third sector) organisations in a particular area act as advocates for individuals to fight or negotiate the system. Citizens Advice Bureau, Voluntary Action Groups etc. will enter confrontational relationships with the local authority, and quite rightly in some cases. However, whilst the fight might be justified it's the system that is wrong, not just the individual case being fought. The council and the third sector are, theoretically at least, on the same side but end up developing adversarial relationships. This means that organisations and departments spend time fighting, negotiating and arguing rather than doing. These same people are then expected to sit nicely round the table later in the week and work closely together. Even the strongest characters amongst us would struggle to build strong relationships with those who have so strongly opposed us. Not that it is impossible, but the 'system of managing through partnerships' impedes rather than promotes close working.

Fundamentally, partnerships bring together organisations and services that are out for what they can get. However public spirited these organisations are everyone fights within the partnership to get the credit, everyone wants the outputs and the achievements, everyone wants their targets and priorities at the top of the list. The partnership programme creates competition rather than an atmosphere of harmony. If our leaders want to create a private sector approach to working they have more than achieved this; it has become a dog-eat-dog world to such an extent that it would make Gordon Gecko blush.

I have lost count of the number of times that I have had my wrists slapped for doing something that has been the common sense thing to do but has upset some partnership or another. I have regularly been told that something I have done is fine in principle but that should have received approval from the appropriate steering group. Emails, telephone calls and face-to-face slanging matches have all been the order of the day with every organisation possible telling me and my colleagues not that we've done the wrong things but that we haven't done them according to the partnerships approach, that an agreement has been broken, that one organisation or another feels that it hasn't received the credit it deserves, that one service is 'taking over'. All fair enough criticism from their point of view but, as we have seen, no one actually wants to do anything. When someone actually gets something done they have put their head over the parapet where it will get shot at.

A Way Forward

The simple truth of the matter is that partnerships on the whole don't work in the way they are intended to. For a long time they have been seen as the ultimate answer for all the woes of the public sector but we need to reflect on their effectiveness. Creating a partnership has now become the automatic response for councils to address just about everything and the sheer number of them should alarm us all. Partnerships have simply become too attractive to council managers because they have the dual benefit of taking away individual responsibility as well as the need to make any decisions whatsoever. They have become a replacement for actually doing the work.

This doesn't mean that partnerships should disappear altogether but rather that they should be used more sparingly, as and when they are needed, rather than as a knee-jerk reaction to every possible situation. Only then will they become effective. Every council up and down the country needs a cull of partnerships, like the national government's 'theoretical' bonfire of the quangos. Partnerships are, after all, nothing more than a type of mini, localised quango.

Killing off the majority of the existing partnerships, changing the attitude that makes partnerships an automatic solution for problems, and removing the partnership support systems that exist in every council is the only sensible way to proceed.

For those partnerships that do remain there is another key criterion that must be adhered to. Those people round the table must use partnerships as an opportunity to actually do some good. Budgets must be pooled for the right projects or pieces of work because it is only when council departments think enough of partnerships to actually contribute money to them, as opposed to just time, that they will do what they are supposed to do. At the moment partnerships are little more than a talking shop for senior officers to nod sagely at and to determine that, "Yes, something really must be done about that." However, currently they are answerable only to themselves and present all involved with a great opportunity to avoid actually doing the things that should be done. They simply pass the buck to some other group in the partnership. If things could be done more efficiently and effectively by officers just doing their job and involving people as and when they are needed then we certainly don't need partnerships to sort things out.

In this case, partnerships are just like project teams...

"There were once four members of a project team: Everyone, Someone, Anyone and No-one. Like all projects there were some important tasks to do. Everyone was really busy and was sure that Someone had more time to do most of these tasks, but Someone thought Anyone could do them. However, Anyone couldn't do them, and so unless Anyone made Someone realise that Someone was the best person to do those jobs, Everyone ended up allocating the jobs to No-one. Sadly No-one wasn't very good at getting these jobs done, so the result was a disaster, which impacted on Everyone. Everyone ended up angry with Someone, because Everyone knew that Someone could do the jobs better than No-one."

6. Planning for the Strategic Strategising Strategists

"Basic skills and sound advice have been replaced by woolly concepts and ideas."

– Frank Chalk

For many large businesses in the real world, strategies are developed in order to help improve their market share. The extent and quality of these strategies varies along with the huge range of businesses that exist in the country. However, the common aim of every strategy is to offer some direction for the future, to outline a plan on how to achieve the ambitions of the shareholders, the management and everyone else involved in that particular business.

The myriad of partnerships that were discussed in the last chapter might give the casual reader a hint at the way that councils adopt strategy development. The strategy approach has been wholeheartedly adopted by councils up and down the country. This has been partly due to central government pressures but, from my experience, it is also partly down to the job creation and work avoidance attitude that is now prevalent in virtually every town hall.

If a Job's Worth Doing…

An old saying suggests that "If a job's worth doing, it's worth doing well." In councils, this sage advice seems to have been appended with, "But if it's not worth doing then write a strategy."

Virtually everything that your council now does, from cleaning the streets to looking after the elderly, requires a strategy to be developed. No longer is it enough just to get on and do stuff. We now need glossy and verbose documents, action plans and policies that describe, at length, the local area, the problem that needs solving, and what the council (and its various partners) intend to do about it.

One reason that these strategies are created is to satisfy the paymasters in central government. In some cases it is a legal or funding requirement for councils to create a strategy, not that this makes it OK to waste thousands of council tax pounds but at least you can see some sort of reasoning behind the work in these cases.

Over and above these legal requirements to produce strategies though, councils have decided that without them no work is worthwhile. While the principle is sound that actions should be prioritised appropriately, that resources are allocated accordingly, unfortunately it doesn't quite pan out like that in the real world.

For those of you out there who haven't had the questionable honour of being involved in creating or using strategies then understandably you may well be asking what on earth they actually are.

The official line from one council suggests that a strategy is a high-level approach to an issue that is designed to deliver change by implementing policy. For a particular subject e.g. housing, regeneration, or community safety, it will set out where we are now, where we are aiming to be in a given period of time, how we plan to get there, and how we will know when we have achieved our goals.

In practice, strategy documents are a real treat for the uninitiated. They invariably consist of rather lengthy documents that take months and months (or in some cases years) to develop. Most have a built in 'best before date' of say three years so after another thirty-six months every department gets to go through the whole charade again.

Most strategies start with a nice, lengthy, and usually pointless consultation exercise and we will see in a moment how well they work. At the end of that officers will have a pile of numbers they can use to tell everyone how shockingly bad one particular problem or another is or how many million people in their town have demanded action yadda, yadda, yadda.

From this initial consultation comes the start of the writing process. In most cases it is something that Mr Dickens himself would be proud of, as officers across the town hall sit down to craft their very own version of *Great Expectations*. Actually that's not quite true; most of Dickens is a very good read. The documents that get spewed out of town halls are neither a gripping read nor a perceptive and incisive plan of action that will leave the reader wanting to know more about how their area is going to get better.

In reality the life's work of many officers in creating these documents turns out to be a bit of a damp squib. Each of them are perhaps thirty of forty pages long (although sometimes up to 200 pages!) and are usually made into glossy 'magazines', which are printed in their hundreds or thousands. Who the target audience is for these brochures is always a mystery to me but suffice to say that they are distributed to that magical group known as 'partners and stakeholders'.

Behind many of the strategies that you will encounter

in your town hall are hundreds of people, processes, and systems that would truly boggle the mind. First, it is worth highlighting that many of these strategies start their life through the work of our good friends – partnerships. To further justify their existence partnerships feel that given that they meet so often and have all the staff in place they might as well show the public just how cutting edge they really are.

Chair: Well everyone, we are in a position where we've been meeting for several months now; we have our terms of reference; we have our admin staff in post and we've issued a press release for each of the previous twenty eight weeks. Perhaps we need to think about really making a difference for our community.

Manager 1: Well, Chair, I've also been thinking about this and have discussed it extensively with my team. As a group have we considered the possibility that in order to make the biggest difference we need to write a strategy to ensure all our actions are joined up?

Manager 2: I have to agree, only by having a strategy can we hope to achieve anything worthwhile.

Chair: So it's unanimous then – we need to create our own strategy to cover Older People's Toenail Cutting. I'd like to propose that we turn to developing an action plan to create this strategy. All in favour say Aye.

And so it all begins: the consultation; the writing; the creation of a draft strategy for consultation; a final version; a launch ceremony. All of this requires many, many hours, and huge amounts of money and resources.

Many councils decide that the creation of some particular strategies are just too much effort and recruit consultants to carry out the work for them. If I were a braver man and had the guts to put my money where my mouth is I'd be setting up a public sector strategy writing consultancy business. At this stage my lawyers have advised me to say that there are some fantastic consultancy companies out there who provide an effective and efficient service. However, there are also just one or two shysters out there who have been known, just on the odd occasion, to take councils for every penny.

These companies are truly onto a good thing. The councils in question collate all the information, tell the company the kind of actions they'd like listing in the strategy and leave them to it for a few months. During this time the consultants do their research (get hold of a few equivalent strategies from other local authorities), write the strategy document up (copy key passages from the internet along with some lovely photographs), and then present the finished product (and their bill).

In fairness this is probably the best way of actually creating these documents as 95% of their content can and should be the same across the board. However, when councils are paying ten, twenty or even fifty thousand pounds for these things I think they should expect a little more than efficient use of Microsoft Word's cut and paste facility.

Throughout the lifespan of strategies council budgets continue to pour unrestrained down the drain. The partnerships (or whatever group) that have created the strategy then, of course, need to monitor its implementation. Again, good in theory; poor in reality. Twenty or thirty managers sat round the table agreeing that the actions have been delivered with outstanding success. They cross things off as they go along, little realising that their strategy has made not one jot of difference. But all is well because they are getting together as a group every two months to monitor things and this can continue for the whole three years of the strategy. More waste; more talk and more reasons why the services are getting worse.

So the strategy has a lifespan of say three years. During this time the usual self-congratulatory back slapping and hype continues amongst those round the table but everyone in the room realises that perhaps they need to be a bit more open and have an 'independent' assessment of their work. So what do they do to prove the success of the strategy? You guessed it: they invite back the same consultants who wrote the strategy to make an independent review of progress.

Please forgive the cynic in me, but I can't help but think that these conversations start something like this:

Council Manager: We'd like to pay you an obscene amount of money in order for you to assess how well we've done implementing the Older Person's Toenail Cutting strategy.

Consultant 1: We'll be there first thing in the morning.

Later that afternoon:

Consultant 2: So they are paying us to assess them. And if we tell them they are great and make the report look good by fudging a few feeble points for improvement they'll think we're great and get us back for more business. But if we assess them properly and tell them how useless they have really been they'll throw a hissy fit, make all sorts of pathetic excuses, tell us we're wrong and never, ever have us back again.

Consultant 1: Er… yes. What do you think we should do then?

Strategy Development Units

"Have you ever seen a five year plan that's says we are going to get worse?"

– Ricardo Semler

OK, so where's the harm in it all? Surely every company needs an action plan about what it is going to do? Dead right. But, just like we have seen previously, the problem with strategies comes not from the principle but from the implementation, the volume of strategies involved and the way that officers and local politicians choose to use them. The planning of services is meant to be detailed, of course – the thousands of people and hundreds of services, it's complicated stuff. But we have reached strategy and action plan overload; documents like this have become all too easy to create but there are just so many of them that no one is able to truly understand them all and pull them together into any semblance of order so they end up having no effective use.

But unfortunately just like the development of partnerships, councils see strategy development as such an important function for the wellbeing of the electorate that they have created specific responsibilities for it in town halls. These departments, teams, or individuals vary from town hall to town hall but all are there to offer advice and support to other services in developing and writing their own strategies. Yes, another team that doesn't actually *do* anything in particular other than help their colleagues. Most of these teams are there to be called in by the various Heads of Service as and when strategies 'need' to be written. They tell managers when they are doing it wrong, tell them how they should look and where they can go for further advice. They collate and log all the strategies that their council has and makes sure that there are plenty of them (after all how else would they have a job) and that they are updated regularly to keep work ticking over nicely. This is another example of a self-sustaining cottage industry.

At this stage I must apologise for lapsing into lists mode but I thought it would be useful to show you an example of what strategies councils actually create on your behalf.

In looking on the website of one particular council, which will remain nameless, I noticed just how accommodating and helpful council officers could be. This particular local authority were so proud of their ability to write documents that they listed every single strategy and policy document that they had written over the last couple of years. The list came to over 160 different ones. Again if the Strategy Development Team are on commission then I think few of us could think of a better use for our tax money then to give these guys a huge bonus.

I'm surely not the only one who thinks this is a little excessive but if you're not convinced multiply that by the number of councils in the country (because the majority are duplicated in each and every local authority area) and the number of hours/pages involved. I reckon between two and four million pages of these things exist at any given time, and trust me, the number is not going down anytime soon. To give you an idea of the importance (or not) of these documents here's just a hundred of the more interesting strategies and policies that may well exist in your own local council (feel free to skip to the end).

Public Engagement

People

Local Preventative

Healthy Ageing

Geographical Information System

End of Life Care

Customer Services

Council-wide Communications

Community Safety

Sustainable Community

Equality

Waste Management

Corporate Parenting

Culture Improvement

Health Improvement and Home Safety

Contaminated Land

Regional Spatial

Economic

Manufacturing

Older People

Sustainability

Anti-Fraud

Conservation

Positive Behaviour in Schools

Empty Property

Homelessness

Transport System

Lesbian, Gay and Bisexual

Sport and Physical Activity

Play

Supporting People

Cycling

ASB

Community Cohesion

Planning Management Improvement

Walking

Employment

Archaeology

Parks and Open Spaces

Procurement and Commissioning

Disability

Primary Strategy Consultation

Adult Carers

Parking

Cultural

Alcohol

Sustainable Schools

Flooding and Erosion

Climate Change

Anti-poverty

Tree

Sustainability

Fathers'

Arts

External Funding

Youth

Playing Pitch

Heritage

Work Life Balance

Biodiversity

Capital

Data Quality

Partnership

Housing & Council Tax Benefit

Local Bus Information

Renewable Energy

Natural Resource Management

Countryside Access

Alley Gating

Allotment

Highway Maintenance

Street Lighting

Cemetery

Street Cleaning

Corporate Enforcement

Air Quality

Volunteering

Bonfire

Back Lane

PESSCL

Travel to School

Obesity

School Modernisation

School Attendance

School Meals

Specialist Schools

Extended School

Stress Prevention

School Investment

School Inclusion

Joint Commissioning

Library

E safety

E procurement

Sustainable Energy

Business Transformation

Signing

International

Parenting

Neighbourhood Renewal

At this stage I'd like to be able to provide you all with a comprehensive review of each of these publications and their role in making the world a better place to live. Sadly I neither had the time nor inclination to read them all and offer a wonderful critique. I work for the council, after all, and am far too lazy to do something so long and laborious. Although in some town hall somewhere I'm sure there is a wizened old man hunched over his desk finishing reading his 157th strategy.

Instead I'll cherry pick a few of the more amusing ones and allow you to make your own mind up from a selection of the pearls of wisdom from up and down the country.

Walking Strategy (Birmingham) – a paltry fifteen-page effort.

"Our hierarchy of users within 'Visions' places pedestrians first where there are choices to be made. Our research shows that there are lots of opportunities for converting at least part of many existing trips to walking. Our commitment to walking and a quality pedestrian environment is reinforced by the views of residents."

Really. The hierarchy of users (whoever that is) have helped to show that perhaps some of the journeys we all make might be walked, that perhaps we should be walking the kids to school instead of driving them round. Phew. Ground-breaking stuff.

"In repeated annual MORI polls of residents' views, street cleaning, road and footpath maintenance and street lighting consistently come out as key service priorities."

Really? So where is "We would like a strategy to get people putting one leg in front of the other more often," on that list?

"A Walking Forum will act as a focus for the development of walking in Birmingham and to drive the implementation of the strategy. This strategy is the first step in making Birmingham a walkable city."

Hurray! The creation of another focus group. Just what's needed to monitor the levels of walking in Britain's second city. As to becoming a walkable city, I appreciate that many cities can be a trial to walk through, but I have yet to visit one where walking is prohibited either by local byelaws or physical limitations like thirty-foot wide chasms and fallen trees.

Newcastle Play Strategy – a more impressive seventy-four page leviathan

"As a result of the consultation process fifteen guiding values and principles [of play] were identified."

Just the fifteen? I can think of at least… er… none. Are we overcomplicating things a bit here? But then of course we are: complicated means volume; volume of pages and of wasteful jobs.

"Objective 7 – To communicate effectively about all aspects of play with the public, including 'hard to reach groups', play providers, internal and external partners and other organisations with the aim of improving the quality of provision and participation."

After reading this for the nineteenth time I decided that it meant that the council would tell residents where the play areas are in Newcastle. Thank goodness. I'm sure the kids, after hunting high and low, can't wait to find out.

Telford Young People's Accessibility Strategy – a healthy forty-one pages

"The Children & Young People's Portfolio (C&YP) is in the process of rolling out a programme of Equality Impact Assessments to evaluate all of its current policies and functions in order to continuously improve the Council's performance in its public duties to promote equality and eliminate discrimination."

At long last. I'm sure the electorate of Telford is heaving a huge sigh of relief as we speak. And they all thought those policies were *never* going to get evaluated. How wrong could they be?

Anyway, I'll stop there before we all lose the will live. You get the idea, though. Basically, these strategies are there to tick a box, to regurgitate the same old rubbish and wheel out ridiculous platitudes and common sense statements dressed up as something profound and ground breaking.

Admittedly, the quotes I have given above are taken in glorious isolation and it is all too easy to take these selected quotes out of context and mock them mercilessly. But the point here is that these few lines are still indicative of the kind of rubbish that is spouted in vast quantities across the country. While none of us can reasonably question the importance of children having somewhere to play, of being able to walk where we wish, or young people being able to access services like everyone else, the creation of a strategy does little, if anything, to actually create better services. It does, however, present managers with the opportunity to rest on their laurels and to tell everyone that they have done all they can.

Contradictions

"Military intelligence is a contradiction in terms."

– Groucho Marx

Sometimes strategic plans do things that are a lot worse than just miss the point, though. In the defence of pointless plans at least they are just that. Pointless. But given the sheer number of strategies that exist in each local area it is probably no surprise that several of them actually end up conflicting with each other.

Take, for example, a conversation I recently had with a friend of mine who works in the health service. He was part of a council partnership which had a strategy that aimed to promote positive health messages to young women. This varied from promoting a healthy diet to reducing drinking levels as well as highlighting the problems of smoking during pregnancy. You know the kind of thing. As always, the strategy was months in development, lots of gimmicky projects resulted and officers spent time patting themselves on the back about how wonderfully well things were going.

One particular winning campaign was to encourage young women out drinking at the weekend to protect themselves from being drugged by local nutters/predators and subsequent sexual attack by ensuring that they never left their drink unattended. So far, so good. Posters went up, leaflets were distributed at all the local drinking dens and everyone in the partnership watched on in expectation. All the strategy meetings highlighted how many leaflets had been handed out, how the posters had raised awareness and how everyone involved in the project deserved a jolly good pat on the back. Until, that is, my friend pointed out that the number of sexual assaults had not changed.

In fact, the women who were receiving this message from the posters and leaflets were finding a new and creative way to ensure that their drinks were never left unattended: they simply necked their drinks quicker in order to make sure they had empty glasses. The result? More binge drinking. The women may not have been drugged but the rate and amount of drinking increased the possibility of assaults occurring. This also has greater health implications in the long term.

Was this phenomenon of unintended consequences investigated and a solution sought? The simple answer is no. The strategy said that they would simply raise awareness of the problem of drinks being spiked; it didn't say anything about binge drinking so it wasn't the strategy's problem. The group had done what it was supposed to do, even if the strategy had impacted negatively on the 'binge drinking strategy'.

And this is another issue with strategies: once written, they become gospel. Of course, the unintended consequences of promoting this warning message would have been hard to predict in advance. I appreciate that. However, the issues that the campaign raised needed to be investigated and a solution found, whatever it was. Unfortunately it wasn't written in the strategy so the fact that it might have created more problems than it solved is irrelevant; the attitude was that the strategy had delivered what it set out to deliver. To look at the feedback is simply not an option, after all it's 'not on the list' is it?

One of my favourite contradictions in strategies (and policies) happened to a close friend very recently. Our council decided to promote the benefits of cycling to work for its employees: the health benefits, the reduction in carbon emissions, less traffic on the road so less congestion etc. Posters went up all over the town hall to encourage everyone to take part and no doubt the Cycling Development Strategy

Group got very excited about how successful they would no doubt be. They even arranged a loan scheme that allowed officers to borrow bikes for this purpose.

My friend decided this was a great opportunity to get involved, to shed a few pounds and help save the world. At the time he was one of the officers who occasionally needed his car for work so he could travel to meet clients or whatever. For this, like everyone else, he was paid an allowance. You'd think then that the best solution would be for Lance to bike to work when he could and take the car when he needed to travel somewhere else to meet people.

But… the Cycling Strategy didn't quite match up to the HR policy. After a few weeks of biking to work Lance received a phone call from HR informing that because there was a requirement under HR policy that all car users 'must have their vehicle at work at all times' then he must find a way of biking to work and getting his car there too, or stop biking to work and come in his car at all times or lose the payments he received for use of his car. Like most people he decided that the car won.

Clearly the idiocy of this story is the HR policy. However, the time, effort, meetings, and marketing costs put into the Cycling Strategy was wasted as officers decided to take the money and the practicalities of their cars over the benefits of cycling.

Just another failed strategy-led project that was pretty much ignored by the Cycling Strategy Group who simply noted in their meeting notes: "Scheme promoted with x number of officer taking up cycling to work." In other words there was no mention of the fact that no one continued to use their bike or that they had pressured HR to change their policy. That, after all, would have been far too hard and the initial uptake was all they were really interested in. Another strategy, then, that looked good in the reports but in reality failed to address what it was meant to address because it came across something that actually took some work to resolve i.e. another set of contradictory policies.

This example might sound pretty small fry, and it is, but if you look around your average local authority there are more subtle conflicts happening all the time between various action plans, strategies and policies. Below are just a few but there a hundred more:

Road Safety Strategy – every council spends thousands on developing safe zones for their schools – signs, barriers, road markings, enforcement and so on. Yet children don't simply exist in the confines of their school. They spend time in other parts of the town or village in which they live. Basically, wrapping the school area in cotton wool does little more than prevent accidents happening around the school (although it is questionable about how much of an issue this really is anyway). Do children start to feel far too safe and start taking risks with how they use roads because they feel everywhere is as safe as their school?

Road accidents near schools are reduced (possibly) = Children's sense of danger when using roads decreased = Number of road casualties remains the same (or increases) but they just happen away from the school area.

Transport policies – a zealous drive to ensure that every main road through our towns has a separate lane for cyclists and traffic 'calming' measures. First, the cycle lanes tend not to be separate; they have a propensity to be on the same bit of tarmac as all the motorists, but they do have a painted white line to keep cyclists safe from various cars, lorries and buses flying past. Meanwhile, the speed bumps slow down traffic to such an extent that the stop-start driving style that is required to overcome these bumps wastes more fuel and flies in the face of the various environmental and climate change strategies that exist.

Increase in number of cycle lanes + increase in traffic calming measures = Questionable safety for cyclists (and pedestrians) + more stop-start driving = No net benefit for cyclists (or pedestrians) + more annoyed motorists + more wasted petrol + more damage to the environment and wasted fuel.

Child Safeguarding Strategies – insistence on protecting children is a good thing. An overriding reliance on checks, checks, and more checks is not. Councils and their partners all insist that staff must be checked for previous criminal convictions by the DBS for any person holding a position that might mean they come into contact with children. From bus drivers to sports coaches, they all have a piece of paper that says they are safe to work with children. Just because the piece of paper says they are it doesn't necessarily make it so. The 'piece of paper' mentality removes the common sense approach as people stop looking for the more subtle signs of improper behaviour with children.

Increases in DBS checks = Greater reliance on an inadequate approach to looking after the needs of children = Reduction in common sense judgements of what is the correct behaviour with children = Children (and parents) in greater danger of not recognising the signs of abuse

Community Development Strategies – all councils aim to increase community pride and spirit by supporting local events, getting residents involved in delivering services, and so on. Many councils also go above and beyond the call of duty when implementing their other strategies and action plans to ensure that licensing laws are implemented to the maximum. There are councils up and down the land who have taken it upon themselves to stop community centre bingo and charity raffles, for example, because the policy says so. There are others that have insisted on such extensive, complicated and expensive licensing applications that village events are cancelled.

Extensive Licensing Policy = Decreased number of unlicensed events = Reduction in the number of community events = Less community spirit = Failure of Community Development strategies

All too often then these strategies, which are designed to help and improve society, end up achieving the exact opposite. Of course, conflicts of interest are always going to arise in this complex world of ours, but councils nail their colours so firmly to the mast that it leaves them with very little room for movement. These conflicts and contradictions, which could be resolved by changes and modifications to the approach taken, become completely insurmountable because of the attitude of 'our strategy must be delivered at all costs'. Case by case judgement of what is the best thing to do becomes the least likely way of doing things.

A Way Forward

"If you don't know what you're talking about you need a strategy."

– Genley Anderson

The emphasis that the public sector places on strategies en masse simply needs exploding. For far too long the creation of a strategy has been seen as the ends rather than (a possible) means. A huge industry has grown up around the creation of these bulky documents, with consultants creaming off a non-too shabby percentage.

Few can argue against the need for a clear direction on where to spend money but when the process of establishing this direction is overly laborious and time consuming then we need to look at an alternative way to decide how funding should be spent.

As with so many other things there needs to be fewer strategies and what remains should be used more effectively. This means throwing out the old and putting in place a clear plan of what each council will do: fewer graphs, fewer glossy pictures, and some simple, straightforward statements of what local people can expect from their local council. We would lose nothing if we disbanded all the strategy development units and left the managers to manage. If and when they need strategic plans then they can do this by themselves. These plans should be practical lists of what they are going to do rather than sexy brochures to impress partnership meetings and focus groups.

We have reached a stage where literally thousands of these things exist. This cull isn't about just getting rid of paperwork it's about changing the culture of 'let's write a strategy' that pervades currently.

By removing the emphasis on these documents we can remove the apparatus for writing them, and staff can actually start to concentrate on the day job. In other words they'll have fewer distractions, fewer overheads, and will have to stop hiding behind the rhetoric of 'look how hard we are working; look how long our strategy is.' With fewer rules, strategies and policies life will start to become easier to understand for all involved and services will become more adaptable to change.

Essentially by removing these documents from the mix council officers and managers will actually start to become more accountable. They will have to come out from behind their desks and start answering questions from the public. No more hiding; no more hype – and instead an explanation of what work is *actually* being done. Just imagine the amount of time and resources that will be saved by not writing and publicising these things, not to mention the number of rainforests that won't have to be chopped down to make these magazines.

Finally, there is another important point to make here. A more subtle change is required from council managers and Whitehall apparatchiks that involves a switch from what some writers call 'strategic planning' to 'strategic thinking'. These are fancy terms but I'd like to think that this means there are fewer plans, paperwork, and strategies, and more responsibility placed on the staff to make decisions, and to adapt and respond to situations as they present themselves – an example of which was given in the librarian example in Chapter 4. By being 'entrepreneurial' in this way and thinking about how specific actions can benefit residents in the wider sense staff will start to see that they don't need strategies to get somewhere. Councils talk about 'joined up' working between services but strategies do nothing to address this.

7. Just Put Your X in the Box

"In the last round of local elections 64% of people declined the right to vote. Of those who did vote few did so in the hope of making a difference locally but rather to support/oppose the national party."

– Douglas Carswell and Daniel Hannan

We have very little say on how the armed services are run or how the police protect us except for the opportunity to vote every five years in the general election. One of the oft-promoted strengths of local government is that it is the easiest opportunity for every resident to get involved in the delivery of public services.

Local government is the best chance for 'real' people to be elected into positions of power. The process of becoming a councillor (called an elected member by some) is relatively straightforward; if you've stayed out of prison for the last few years, if you can get ten people to agree to sign a sheet of paper in support, if you don't work for the council and if you actually want to be elected then you've got a real chance; you just need to pick your party, let them interview you to check you haven't got two heads, and off you go. Congratulations, you've entered politics.

Fingers then need to be firmly crossed approaching local election day as the electorate go out in their thousands (well hundreds) to put their cross in the box. But if you're a little bit nervous in your first election, don't be. Most ward elections have at least two or even three seats up for election (meaning between thirty and seventy seats in each local authority) and given the complete indifference of the vast majority of the electorate, councillors can be elected to the town hall with just a few hundred votes. Many people in local elections still simply vote for their chosen party rather than the individual so you can stay pretty relaxed as long as you have picked the right party and the right ward. (A nice affluent rural ward for the blues and a deprived inner city one for the reds, as a general rule of thumb.) So – welcome to the town hall, 'Councillor'.

The structure of democracy in the town hall is a curious one. The average local council has a worryingly large number of councillors elected to oversee things. Parliament has around 650 MPs overseeing the lives of every aspect of 60 million people – that's one MP for every 80,000 people or so. In local government an authority area of 100,000 people might have more than fifty elected officials – one councillor for every two or three thousand people.

Commentators often discuss the size of national government and suggest that 650 MPs are far too many to run the country. What implications might this then have for the number of local councillors in town halls, given that there are well over twenty thousand of them in the country?

The argument for a reduction in the number of councillors is not about critiquing the role of democracy in a modern society. This is a discussion for another day and another book. There are far more pragmatic reasons for questioning the merit of having this number of members kicking their heels in town halls.

First, each and every elected member receives an

element of support from 'Democratic Services' teams. These teams, made up of mostly administrative staff, are there to help councillors (who admittedly often have full time jobs of their own) manage their calendars, sort out correspondence, minute meetings etc. Effectively, they act as PAs to the councillors. So it doesn't take a rocket scientist to see some obvious waste in the system. Fewer councillors means less support is required.

But this argument is a little simplistic; it's easy to see waste everywhere when we simply say that there should be less of everything. By this notion, waste can be reduced by randomly sacking one out of every ten people working at the town hall. Tempting though this approach may be to some people it simply isn't practical because it takes no account of the value provided by the councillors in question.

Your Elected Members

"Government is very important; I've just never met anyone who's doing it."

— *Yes Minister*

So what do these elected members actually do? Looking through a variety of websites I'm still not sure but here are some of the more choice nuggets I have been able to extract from one particular local authority.

A councillor's first duty is to represent the people of the ward in which they are elected. This will include promoting the ward's interest at council meetings and helping people with particular problems in relation to council services.

This is a key element that many of the elected members I work with seem to have forgotten. In practice, this work is usually done by councillors who are not in power.

Our local authority, for example, is a Labour led one and is effectively run by four or five of the most hard line councillors who convince, cajole and threaten their colleagues into accepting their way of doing things. These bully boys (and girls) do little, if anything, to represent the people within their part of the county; they are far more concerned with exerting their power than helping their wards. Where councillors do help their ward it is usually more about grabbing a few votes than achieving the greater good for their ward.

Councillors are asked for advice on anything from obtaining a home help service to the availability of a housing warden's service. They also gain knowledge of other services and organisations which they can use to help people.

The key phrase here is 'help people' and a number of the councillors I work with entered local politics to do just that. Sadly, they are in a minority. The rest joined for a variety of reasons that I shudder to think of but the good old-fashioned ethic of doing something for your fellow man seems in short supply in council chambers up and down the land.

At meetings of the council, and any committees dealing with specific services, a councillor will also have a responsibility to consider not only issues which benefit the ward they represent but also the whole of the Borough.

I write more about 'meetings of the council' later in the book. In short, however, there are a very small minority of councillors who make decisions based on the facts and information in front of them. Many seem to think this unusual; after all, what's wrong with making your mind up first and then simply interpreting the facts in a way that suits?

Under the direction of the Leader, some councillors are given responsibility for delivering services in a particular field, called their 'portfolio'.

Local councillors know they've made it when they are given a portfolio to manage. These portfolios present plenty of opportunity for press releases, quotes in local papers and even snippets on local television. What self-respecting publicity seeker wouldn't want this opportunity? Being a portfolio holder or other senior member of the council means that *you* make the decisions; for some this is a responsibility that makes them rise to the challenge for others it serves to inflate their egos to an extent that they could have only dreamed of before they entered local politics.

As a councillor you could also be involved in many other areas, such as Neighbourhood Management Schemes and representing the council on outside bodies, such as Police, Fire and charitable organisations.

This presents the good councillors even more opportunity to make a difference in their local community, contributing to positive change. For the hangers on it's an even better opportunity to fluff up their feathers and to look more important. For the downright cynical councillors it's an opportunity for extra payments, allowances and TV appearances.

The Usual Suspects

"Politicians are the same all over. They promise to build a bridge even where there is no river."

– Nikita Khrushchev

Reading my initial comments on local democracy you would be forgiven for thinking that I have little respect for local politicians. To a certain extent I can't argue differently. While I have met some fantastically committed and capable elected members they are very few and far between.

In my experience, far from being a collection of talented individuals who fight hard on local issues, many councillors are there for other reasons. From my experience, our elected representatives fall into one (or occasionally more) of the following categories:

The Champions – there for the right reason, to do their bit to help the community. Champions tend to claim less allowances, appear in the newspaper less and are well respected by the majority of hard working council officers and local residents. They do not pander to public opinion per se; they make decisions based on their best judgement. This might be wrong on occasion but the principles stand strong. They are great to work with, but only if you are willing to work hard and build a good relationship with them. They won't let any officers hide.

The Egomaniacs – these individuals are the 'Big I Ams' who feel that they are the lifeblood of local politics and things would be worse without them. They are most clearly identified by the number of times they appear in the local rag and the number of quotes they give to anyone who'll listen about any particular subject. The Egomaniacs, by definition, crave power. They have worked their way up to the top of their particular party and hold senior positions or have their own portfolio. Their allowances are usually fully claimed because as the advert states, 'they're worth it'. Occasionally a canny operator will refuse his/her allowances if there is some publicity to be gained from that approach. These people will step on anyone in their way.

The Invisibles – these are the councillors who *nobody* knows. They only appear at feeding and voting time.

Expenses are invariably claimed, decisions are avoided, as are press stories because that way someone might identify them and they'd have to answer tricky questions. Decisions are taken based on the answer to 'what is the least controversial?' They will become the Duracell Bunnies of the future if they manage to stay hidden for long enough. I have no idea if they are easy to work with; I've never had the chance to meet one.

The Crooks – enough said really. Whether consciously or not, these individuals never, ever lose out on a deal which the council might be involved in. Naturally, allowances are claimed to the penny but press stories are shunned in case it attracts attention to them and their other activities. They invariably stay on the right side of 'legal' even if what they are doing is morally questionable. They get on with most people but hate anyone who might rumble their extracurricular interests.

The Duracell Bunnies – the last stage for most elected members. These councillors have been part of the council for longer than the town hall they meet in. These are the councillors who have sat on every committee and were attending important meetings "Before you were in long trousers, young man." This group are easy to get on with and are harmless enough but still manage to block seats that the otherwise more worthy candidates might be able to fill. They claim every last penny they are entitled to (why else be a councillor?) but rarely appear in the papers; they would be happy to support public campaigns but only if that doesn't mean missing lunch. Decisions are based on tradition rather than facts. Note the similarities with The Invisibles (above).

The Young Pretenders – there are a small number of

'new to politics' councillors who have yet to be truly sullied by local democracy. They are on the whole nice people who still believe that they can make a difference in their community. They are keen, eager and naive but probably destined, because of the system, to fall into one (or more) of the other categories I have listed. They tend to appear a lot in the newspapers simply because they think it's the 'done thing'. Whether or not they claim every last penny of allowances depends upon who in their party advises them.

The Scarecrows – this is the miscellaneous group. These are people who have yet to decide why they put their names up for election. They often have no idea what they stand for, if anything, and fail to fully grasp what's going on. They have a heart, and sometimes principles, but lack the ability to actually put it all together. If they had a brain they'd either be dangerous or fantastic. They are not organised enough to claim everything they can or to pick and choose the right press stories to appear in, but Scarecrows occasionally appear to be Champions more through good luck than good management. They are easy to get on with because they want to make some friends who might be able to give them some useful ideas.

Party Games

"The more you observe politics, the more you've got to admit that each party is worse than the other."

– Will Rogers

We all have our own perceptions of how party politics at the national level really works. We all know that the Labour, Conservative and Liberal Democrat parties have clear political differences on hundreds of different issues; that the individuals who represent them also have different political ideologies and, theoretically at least, they do not make for comfortable bedfellows. We hear an almost daily barrage of insults, name calling and blaming taking place in the media as they try to score political points off each other.

But the more cynical and realistic of us also know that behind the veil of animosity and hatred there is a respect and camaraderie. Perhaps it is a begrudging one but it exists all the same. Naturally this is not the case between every individual, but the fact is that deals get done and compromises get made in the smoke-filled halls of Westminster. One party whip talks to another, one party leader shares their ideas with another, all in order to get legislation passed, to get *something* done.

This way of working isn't necessarily about the individuals who do the negotiating backing out on their principles or the manifesto they were elected on. It is something far more practical and down to earth than that. It is about the politicians realising that without negotiation and deal brokering nothing can ever happen. Little enough really happens in politics, but without the secret handshakes then we'd be at a standstill.

So what then of our elected heroes in local government? What political arrangements do they come to behind closed doors? Well, I have to concede the answer to this is virtually none. Local councillors are so entrenched in their own political parties that the very idea of compromise is abhorrent to them. There are no deals, few conversations and very little respect. Councillors simply take every opportunity they can to play party politics through petty name calling and cheap sound bites. Check out your local newspaper; every council story will contain quotes from councillors sticking blindly to their national party line irrespective of the local context or meaning.

Some people out there may be thinking, 'Well, good on them,' for standing so resolutely to their principles. This is an understandable point of view and one I must admit to having when I first started working with elected members. The first Labour councillor I worked closely with was a diehard unionist and would rather have poked his own eyes out than so much as have a coffee with 'one of those Blue Bastards'. His hatred and passion was truly awesome. His party allegiances clouded his every step, conversation and decision.

Mr Red is not alone in this; I have seen very, very few instances of councillors working together and, frankly, the petty party divides at a local level are utterly pointless and very damaging to the wider electorate. The cleaning of streets, the inspecting of food preparation establishments and the provision of leisure centres and libraries does not need party politics. Not at a local level at least. We can argue at a national level about policies and all the rest but local authorities are about making *local* decisions and making the best choices for their residents.

Local issues, while not always easy to solve, are crying out for an agreed local solution. It is at the local level then that the biggest differences can be made and it is very important that the people in authority can find common ground as opposed to finding things to disagree on.

But local politics brings out the worst in the Egomaniacs. They are not able to make the big, national decisions that that they crave and so instead take the opportunity to chuck their weight around at every possible opportunity, just like the 'Little Hitlers' who exist in every organisation.

Whilst sat in the office of one Labour councillor, after they had recently taken control of the authority in the local elections, I saw the real attitudes within party politics at play. The councillor (let's call him Mr Silverback) was a senior member of the party and the classic Egomaniac type. One of his colleagues (a Young Pretender) came to speak to him and asked about who would be able to attend the next meeting of some partnership or another with him. The YP suggested that it was worth asking one of the Tory councillors (Councillor Champion) who was something of a local expert on the subject in question and had been involved previously.

Mr Silverback's response was something to behold. Standing up from his chair, he glared at the YP, who seemingly cowered in front of him, for a few seconds sneered, and then said simply in his growling tone, " Champion's a f–ing Tory. The Tories are gonna get f– all while we're in power. The Blue Bastards don't get invited to meetings, don't get any f–ing information and we don't f–ing talk to them unless it's to tell them how f–ing s–t they are."

A truly wonderful example of joined-up, grown-up working, then. If they had conversations like that in front of a fairly junior officer like me imagine what they say in the privacy of their own clandestine party meetings. This may sound like an extreme example and the amount of bile may be unusual but the animosity happens all day every day. Point scoring is the name of the game and pressing home any slight advantage you may have is crucial. What happens to services and the local voters during these bickering matches is of little or no concern to them.

Don't get me wrong, I know that people don't get on. I know that in your average company the Head of Marketing might not see eye to eye with the Head of Planning, that the Head of Production might have run off with the wife of the Head of Development. But these are personal differences, not an institutionalised hatred and mistrust where individuals are taught and encouraged to disagree for the sake of it as standard practice.

In the private sector you are likely to get the same types of people but the average company doesn't have a collection of twenty people who each vote for who is going to be Head of Marketing or Production. In local authorities by default most of the 'types' rule themselves out of the running for the senior positions: Invisibles, Duracells, Scarecrows etc., so we end up with Egomaniacs and a smattering of Champions in charge of the direction of councils across the country. Most of these people have got to the top of their party through scoring political points from the opposition, and if that's what gets them to the top then why would they stop once they are in a position of power?

So councils are led by people who are out for themselves and the party first and the local community second. This, of course, is a reflection of the national picture; few could dispute that. But it all seems more sordid at the local level; it is more like your neighbour lying to you rather than some bigwig in Westminster telling giant porkies.

"Politics is the art of looking for trouble, finding it everywhere, diagnosing it incorrectly and applying the wrong remedy."

– Groucho Marx

But these descriptions of mine I fear are all too dry and rambling. The best thing for any of you out there to do is to attend a council meeting. They really are a joy to behold and have to be seen to be believed.

TV cameras were first allowed into the House of Commons more than twenty-five years ago and local councillors seem to have used the previous two decades to perfect their stagecraft. And I use the term 'stagecraft' quite deliberately because these monthly AmDram productions all too often become slanging matches; this is where the MPs of the future cut their political teeth, learning to name call and harangue the opposition.

The party wannabes certainly take advantage of their brief time in the limelight. If you have seen the paper waving and booing that takes place in the Commons then you'll have some idea of how it all works. These local political heroes do not have quite the same sense of timing, nor the personality or intelligence of the majority of their Westminster counterparts, but you will experience two or three hours of barracking, blame laying and pathetic innuendo all in the name of improving public services. Without the 'calming' influence of a speaker, these meetings are very much like playground skirmishes each side believes they have scored points based solely on who comes up with the most amusing nickname for the other gang's leader. Certainly nothing useful is achieved.

The classic comebacks in council meetings are invariably party based and not issue based. I have heard a Tory councillor counter a formal Labour councillor's question on policy with the statement, "Well, the Labour Party don't have the right to ask that question after the way they ran things round here." The Labour councillor then stood up to ask the question again and was told by one of the clerks at the meeting that "No secondary questions are allowed."

I have also been in attendance when the leader has suspended a full council meeting of fifty people for half an hour to ask advice on whether a specific question can be asked at a specific time or if it needs to be tabled at a later date.

Once again I realise I was being hopelessly optimistic when I went to my first council meeting with the vague hope that it would be a collection of interested, committed individuals discussing the merits of different approaches to service delivery. Sadly, it is always a case of 'we're the ruling party, the rest of you can stick it, and that's the way it is until the next election.' In most of the authorities where I have worked the next election made absolutely no difference as certain parties could have put a shaved monkey up in some wards and still have guaranteed themselves a majority. Is this really the democratic discourse and accountability the ancient Greeks held in such high esteem?

Another demonstration of the 'party before the electorate' is demonstrated in the blogs, tweets and media quotes that stem from elected officials. They always amuse me because there is actually so little of the individual councillor involved in what they write. Party lines are firmly toed (often to the detriment of local issues) simply to ensure the individual councillor continues to get their milk and cookies from party HQ. The cut and paste facility of the digital age must be one of the most overused ones in the modern world. Some party councillors share the text of their personal tweets with each other, party spin from headquarters is copied straight into tweets to ensure that the electorate get the consistent message and 'quotes' for the press from individual councillors go through three or four party officials to get sign off. It's all like a mini Westminster production and it all detracts from making local issues the most important thing.

So whether it is day-to-day dealings, public meetings, or the spin that gets spewed out, the message from our locally elected champions is invariably the same: local decisions will be based on what our masters at party headquarters tell us and in the absence of a direct answer from our party headquarters we will default to the generic party stance.

As far as the electorate goes, this approach has little or no place even in Westminster and so to see it in hundreds of town halls in this day and age is frankly appalling. After all, decisions on smaller local issues are still very important to the residents of the area and most certainly do not need a political slant. That's what national politics is for.

Paying the Price

"Power tends to corrupt, and absolute power corrupts absolutely. Great men are almost always bad men."

– Lord Acton

National stories on MPs expenses have served to illustrate the benefits that certain individuals can extort from the democratic system. I have already touched upon what council staff can screw out of the system, but things can be equally cushy for the average elected member in your local town hall.

First, it is important to note that, unlike MPs, councillors do not get paid.

Instead, councillors receive an 'allowance'. The exact difference between an allowance and a wage is... er... erm... I have no idea. However, there are several advantages of the allowance system. The first is that it allows the publicity-seeking councillors to say, "I don't get paid for this you know," at every available opportunity.

The second advantage is that the level of allowances is set locally rather than nationally. In short, the people in power get to decide how much the people in power can claim. This is one of the few actual decisions local authorities get to make; although with lots of guidance from above, of course.

My local authority, for example, has decided that every single elected member has a basic allowance of just over £12,000. This varies between unitary authorities and I have seen as little as £6,000. Basic is the operative word here though as they can claim this for each of their four years in office, whether they do anything or not.

OK, admittedly that's not a huge amount, but

remember many of them already have a day job and being a councillor is not intended to be a full time job. It is not meant to be thirty-seven plus hours a week, although a number of councillors do work for that long and more.

The good news for councillors is that beyond the basic allowance payments there are numerous other payments that can be claimed to 'top up' the housekeeping money. Special Responsibility Allowances are paid for special responsibilities. This can include everything from being Party Leader through to the chairing of meetings, being the Biscuit Monitor or Member In Charge of Staple Supplies (OK, I'm being facetious, but you get the drift). In my current authority twenty-nine out of fifty-six councillors receive these extra allowances. This ranges from around £1,000 for being a part time Executive Member (who knows?!) all the way up to £25,000 for the Leader.

Your own councillors' allowances and claims should all appear on your local council's website and will hopefully make some interesting reading. After everything is taken into account (meeting attendance bonuses, mileage (including if they travel on their bike!), and meal costs) some of our senior councillors 'earn' more than £40,000 a year. Not bad for a job that doesn't pay anything.

Now if I was able to ignore *everything* that I've written in the rest of this chapter about councillors then I have to admit that on principle I wouldn't have a problem with councillors earning £50K, £80K or even £100K. However, the fact is that too many hide behind the 'I'm not paid for this' platitude.

The actual savings to be made from a root and branch review of things would be fractions of a percent of council budgets. However, there is a principle at stake here and the monetary value is actually secondary compared to the positive message it would send out to the electorate that the whole system is being made more effective.

I want you to jump… how high sir?

"Politicians like to panic; it's their substitute for achievement."
— *Yes, Prime Minister*

The relationship between councillors and officers is one that amuses and shocks me in equal measure. In theory it should be one of mutual trust and respect. In practice it is more like a game with very strict rules.

The first thing to remember is that the councillor doesn't actually work for the electorate directly. They work for the party first and foremost; every decision they make and conversation they take part in has one overriding thought: what would be best for the party? And if this happens to be what's best for the electorate then everyone's a winner.

The second thing to bear in mind is how little power the average councillor actually has. In any given council the power will rest with perhaps five or six senior party members. These are the Egomaniacs and Champions of earlier. So if there are forty or more councillors at least thirty of them have little or no say in the running of the authority; their primary role is simply to support the five or six at the top at the public voting sessions. Occasionally, the lesser councillors are given an unimportant job to do like chairing a meeting. Their mandate is to ensure that the opposition party don't get a say, don't get their way and, hopefully, disappear into the background.

But even the senior politicians don't have that much power. As we have seen in other chapters central government hold *all* the aces and make all of the big decisions, set the direction and dish out the money. This leaves the local leaders in a situation where they have one hand tied securely behind their back. The result is that they swing and fight twice as hard with the hand that they do have free.

They will squeeze out every last drop of power that they do have, approving projects which ensure that they appear on the front page of the local rag and micro managing the basic duties of officers. This level of micro managing highlights their propensity for feeling important – it is they who have made the decisions and no one else.

I have been criticised several times in the past by councillors who feel that I have overstepped the mark and made decisions that they should have made. Sorry to bring up more meetings but one such criticism came from a lead member who called my boss to express his concerns about me. What was my crime? I had booked a room for a meeting at a venue that the member in question hadn't approved. The result? Book a new venue of which he did approve; inform twenty people and use up half a day of the councillor's assistant's time to redo all the paperwork. I can only apologise now for my gross dereliction of duty in second-guessing such an important decision and getting it so hideously wrong.

In fairness, my colleagues have also been caught out on this one so I didn't feel as guilty as perhaps I could. But this incident is the tip of a very repetitive iceberg as councillors rattle their sabre on a regular basis. Talking to colleagues who work directly for councillors these kinds of thing happen on an almost daily basis over some inane issue or another. In fairness, my colleague isn't too bothered as all; the repetition and reorganising means that they stay in a job.

While the interest they take in the daily tasks being carried out by officers is admirable the way in which everything must be approved by them is little more than muscle flexing on their part. It serves as a reminder to officers and the electorate that they are in charge.

My first director in local government gave me this sage advice that he told me would stand me in good stead for the future. It was basically the good old management standby of treating people (or in this case, councillors) like mushrooms: keep them in the dark and feed them on bullsh–t.

The same director was true to his philosophy throughout my time in his department. Every member of his team likely to have any day-to-day dealings with councillors was told in no uncertain terms that we were not to talk directly to them without his approval. This would avoid any 'mixed messages' being passed out of our department. Every email to a councillor first had to be approved by the director (or his PA in his absence) before it could be sent and each meeting we had with an elected member had to be pre-empted with a briefing from the director to ensure that whatever was discussed could be scripted beforehand. Imagine it, a man on £60,000 checking the individual emails of junior staff to ensure we didn't say the wrong thing to the wrong person and preparing 'scripts' for us all to stick to when dealing with the people meant to be managing £200 million of public money. Something somewhere is very wrong indeed and so there is little wonder that some councillors resort to micro-management.

Three bags full

"Many of the ills of local authorities stem from the quality of councillors; people of such modest abilities controlling such large organisations… J S Mill wrote in 1861 of the low calibre of men in local government."

– J A Chandler

One of the least appealing character traits councillors have is their propensity for supporting local causes. I am referring to the hidden incidents that don't quite tug on the heartstrings as much as, say, an orphanage story would. These local causes often start as a result of a phone call from an irate resident. One such example was given to me by a colleague who works in the council enforcement team and is responsible for issuing fines to people who illegally fly tip their rubbish. Whether you agree or disagree with the principle of a council officer rooting through rubbish to determine who dumped it, fly tipping is illegal and costs thousands of pounds to clear up. Many councils issue fines to discourage offenders.

My colleague told me of one resident who was caught after dumping twenty or thirty bags of rubbish in a country lane. Almost every bag contained evidence of where it had come from (cue a stream of letters from lawyers here decrying 'stitch-up' and 'circumstantial evidence only'). Upon receipt of his fine, however, this gentleman (let's call him Mr Wright) had an inspirational idea. Rather than deny it, front it out, take it through the courts or even just pay up, he made one phone call – to his ward councillor.

All Mr Wright said to his councillor was that according to his research more people had been fined in his ward than any other in the county and that clearly this was a case of victimisation. Was the councillor going to stand for this? Or was he going to tell the officers in question that they were being unreasonable? That very same day the councillor called in at the office and demanded to go through all the figures for where fines had been issued in the last two years. For nearly an hour he sat leafing through paperwork, tutting and asking questions. After that he simply handed the papers back to my colleague and went up to see the service director.

Mr Wright received a personal visit at home from the service director early that evening to apologise for the distress our fine had caused and an assurance that the fine had been cancelled. My colleague was reminded that we operate in a political environment and that perhaps he should be working harder to fine offenders from other parts of the county. In fact, perhaps for the next few months he should not issue fines in the particular ward Mr Wright lived in; after all, it wouldn't look good for our service to be seen to be prejudiced against a particular area, would it?

"A government which robs Peter to pay Paul can always depend on the support of Paul."

– George Bernard Shaw

Councillors also seem willing to pick up on passing whims and will start to champion virtually anything that comes their way. Knowing that twenty or thirty votes in some areas can make the difference between being elected and being a no-one inspires councillors to take on some very strange campaigns. Anyone who makes a complaint against an officer or a department is taken seriously even if his or her issue is proven to be unfounded. Holding hands and hugging the electorate – even if their opinions are hideously out of kilter with the real world – means votes for councillors. Telling them to go away and stop being unreasonable doesn't seem to register as an option. But saying, "Yes sir, no sir, three bags full sir," doesn't mean that we are being accountable in any real way.

This is where the local picture seems to reflect all the worst parts of national politics. Anyone who has the ear of an elected member has pretty much the same sabre rattling capacity as the councillors themselves. The number of hours some of my staff and I have wasted on various goose chases initiated by councillors and their friends from the lodge is hair-raising. I swear I have had teams of front line workers spending hours walking down miles and miles of country lanes looking for half a bag of kitchen rubbish that has been photographed and reported by a close friend of a councillor. The location along with a description of the rubbish it seems would have made our jobs just too easy. Cue a Keystone Cops style chase across Britain's green and pleasant land.

If you think that this is harmless enough just remember that every minute spent looking for a stray crisp packet outside the house of one of the councillor's friends is a minute not spent on more important tasks. These pointless tasks create financial waste as staff are taken away from their duties, and a sense of injustice from the committed staff. They see that the majority of local residents don't quite get the same call on services that the councillors do.

A Way Forward

"Democracy must be something more than two wolves and a sheep voting on what to have for dinner."

– James Bovard

There are a few steps that we as a nation should be able to take to address some of the issues I have highlighted. The first for me is to take the party politics out of the town hall. This sounds like a tall order, but if the mind is willing...

Political parties create their policies and manifestos at a national level and this is the inherent problem. Local politicians, almost without exception, find it very hard (as anyone would) to truly relate national policies to local issues. How can a right-wing philosophy for a free market really help when councillors are deciding about closing an old people's home? The automatic response of outsourcing to the private sector, for example, might not be the best way in every particular case. Similarly, a left-wing approach might not be the overall answer either. Basically, many local issues need local knowledge and more importantly the freedom to make the right decision in each respective case without being hamstrung by the fact that the right solution for that particular area might differ from national policy.

In short, if an old folks home needs selling off to the highest bidder then that decision should be made based on local opinion, the financial situation, the potential benefits etc. and not on whether the party high command in their ivory tower feels that it might send out the wrong message.

All councillors should stand on their own merit without the backing of a party. Their manifesto would be based on their CV, their personal skills and their opinions rather than being elected on the back of the national party. This would make the individual responsible for the decisions, and not the party. In one fell swoop the political motivations of councillors would be removed. Naturally, people would still have personal allegiances and would form alliances but this approach would limit the power of the party and force individuals to work together to make decisions rather than running to their colour corner when things get tough. Naturally this approach will create its own problems. With a collection of disparate individuals and views there is the potential for stalemate at every step. However, if the rules of governance are set up correctly that problem shouldn't become an issue.

One thing that would help to lower the incidence of potential stalemate is a reduction of the number of councillors out there. By having twenty councillors in an area instead of fifty, the Duracells and the Invisibles can be dispensed with and there is much, much less room for people to hide. If decisions aren't made or mistakes happen then the buck can only be passed so far. With fifty-odd people it is so much easier to disappear into the background and simply soak up the allowances.

This step is not just about saving money; it is about making the system work in a far more effective way. With little more than a dozen places for councillors and no political party to hold their hands many councillors will begin to realise that local 'politics' is not the place for them, and the hangers-on will hopefully start to disappear. Councils will be made up of Champions, Egomaniacs and Young Pretenders – not a perfect combination but with less of a political quagmire to wade through they will at least have a fighting chance of making things work.

As to the other problems discussed in this chapter these are more difficult to address directly. The hope is that if competition for councillor places is really stepped up then the quality would improve, and if councillors are actually allowed to make important decisions themselves, rather than having one hand tied behind their back, then decision makers would step up to the plate and if the political backbiting is removed the independent businessman, achiever, or academic will feel more willing to get involved.

There are dozens and dozens of people in local communities who are willing and able to step up to the plate. You only have to look at how a controversial development in a town or village throws up outraged groups who campaign tirelessly against things. Whether they are NIMBYs or not, there is usually at least one individual who stands out as intelligent, community minded, and more than able to become a successful non-political councillor. These are the ones who should be attracted into local government.

All this sounds like a hopeless situation but something seriously needs to change with the system of local elections. The national government need to grasp the nettle and actually make significant alterations rather than simply tweaking county boundaries or creating new codes of conduct for councillors.

8. Can You Spare a Moment to Answer a Few Questions, Sir?

"You do not open up to a national debate until the government has privately made up its mind."

– *Yes, Prime Minister*

One of the buzz words to spring up over the last few years in councils and the public sector more generally is 'consultation'. The idea of involving local residents in how their own services are delivered is one that few people could argue against in principle. It's our money; the services are for us so we should therefore have lots of say in how things are done – a lot more than a general election every five years and local elections every four years anyway.

For local councils in these modern times it is extremely important that we talk to our local electorate on a regular basis, on virtually every possible topic and at extreme length. Consultation has become such a strong driver of services that no project, scheme, change or anything else can start without an exercise to discover what local people think of things.

The main drive for consultation comes from our friends at Whitehall. The last few years have seen more and more emphasis being placed on delivering services *for* local people rather than *to* local people. The difference is subtle but basically it means that Whitehall wants councils to stop delivering services based purely on what officials in the town hall think and start to listen to what the voters want.

An admirable aim, I am sure you would agree. Sadly, this fine notion is then picked up by council officials who manage to take it from something worthwhile and meaningful towards the comical and pointless in two or three hundred easy steps.

What Does It Mean?

"One fifth of people are against everything all of the time."

– Robert Kennedy

Consultation means different things to different people, particularly those who work at the town hall. My current local authority, for example, runs the full gamut of attitudes from the old school approach of, "Let's just get the bloody job done; does it really matter what Joe Public wants?" to the wonderful, touchy-feely new school of, "We can't possibly decide this without a full public consultation; we're here to serve the community so must have the public input."

The majority of staff in the town hall sit somewhat uncomfortably in the middle not really sure what they need to consult on and what they don't. Reams and reams of guidance have been produced by councils as well as by the national government to outline just how we are supposed to talk to our electorate.

Most of us are probably very familiar with planning consultations whether it is a request to build a conservatory on the back of your neighbour's house or a multi-million pound development to create a new shopping centre. Virtually all building work that takes place needs to be publicised to local people so that they can express their views and the correct decisions will ultimately be made in the interests of the local community.

This publicising to the local community and seeking their opinion is the consultation phase. It might consist of a sheet nailed to a lamppost or a few leaflets sent out to local houses asking people to contact the council if they object to the development. Naturally, most conservatories get few complaints and shopping centres bring out everyone with any kind of opinion on the rights and wrongs of urban development.

Consultation on planning matters is now well established in the public psyche. There are perhaps as many critics as supporters in the way that it works. The speed at which decisions are made for example often frustrates those involved. If you want to change any aspect of your house the wait for 'approval' can certainly be somewhat lengthy. It seems that fast tracking 'no-brainers' through the consultation phase is rarely an option.

But planning consultation is the tip of an immense iceberg when it comes to involving the public. Whenever a new approach, project or service is being launched, or changed (even in a small way) those in charge feel the need to launch a consultation exercise. Invariably this is not a small job. Let's assume as an example that a council partnership wants to create its very own strategy. First of all they'll need to consult on its content. This means that they first of all select something that those around the table perceive as a problem – let's for the sake of argument say underage drinking.

From here they decide on a consultation plan to

establish what the need is. Questionnaires are sent out to schools to find out many young people have been drunk; residents are surveyed to establish how much of a problem drunken youths are in their neighbourhood; statistics are collected from A&E on the number of admissions of young people due to alcohol, and so on. The results are collated and a few ideas suggested that allow more consultations to be carried out. This might be more surveys, visits to local schools by a team of officers, events where the public are invited along to establish opinion and the good old focus group where local residents are invited to meetings to discuss their ideas and thoughts. If the group are feeling particularly hi-tech they might even carry out online consultations.

The methods of consultation vary, and so does the scale. However, the theory is always the same: ask the public (or at least some of them) what they think of a particular issue, project or idea, and then this allows the decision-making process to be based on delivering what the public actually want.

The theory sadly falls down when it comes to practice though. I have been involved in dozens and dozens of public events aimed at getting residents talking to council officials about one thing or another. While a handful have been well-attended, well-structured and produced positive results, the majority have been a long way from this. Far too many have involved six or seven officers sat on their own in the middle of a community centre chatting about the weather and surrounded by expensive display boards showing plans for a new road layout or whatever. These events sometimes last for days and at the very least for hours. Occasionally they may be interrupted by a random passerby out walking their dog and wondering what is going on – or even less occasionally by a local resident who got the flyer through their letterbox and was interested enough to come and ask questions.

Council officers invariably outnumber members of the public at these events and while some contentious issues do attract larger numbers these are few and far between. For every worthwhile and well-attended event there are twenty pointless, wasteful ones. I'm actually embarrassed at these events, when residents do attend I invariably find myself apologising for the poor organisation or lack of other people. How can anyone take a consultation exercise seriously in a dusty, deserted village hall where one old lady gets pounced on by half a dozen keen and eager officers as she walks through the door looking for the bingo session in the next room? Staff are this eager because they are just delighted to see a new face after three hours of unbelievable boredom reading their own leaflets and posters.

Taking It Too Far...

"Local authorities spend vast sums on seeking opinions from those who have little or no interest in, or first-hand knowledge of, their services. Such surveys can only yield unreliable data and invalid conclusions."

– John Seddon

The modern take on consultation has started to take the all familiar local authority approach of, "This is a good idea; let's apply it to every single thing we ever do." As part of my day job I have often spoken to my manager (or the relevant councillor) to decide how to progress a particular project and the default answer invariably given to me is to carry out some public (or user group) consultation. That way the decision and the results that stem from the chosen course of action are not the council's fault. Although of course if things go well then it's only fair that we as a local authority get the credit for making the correct decision.

On the face of it surely no one can have a problem with this. Local authorities are answerable to the local electorate and so shouldn't the local electorate decide what work is carried out? Of course this is a notion that is hard to disagree with, but when it comes down to brass tacks is it is simply not practical to get everyone's opinion on every single decision.

Even when consultation is carried out it is debatable whether the answers that are received really have any value. This doesn't mean that public opinion doesn't matter – far from it. It simply means that for public opinion to be used properly it should be fully informed and utilised in conjunction with a number of other factors to arrive at the right decision.

My colleagues tell me of an example in one nearby local authority. A few years ago that council were awarded hundreds of thousands of pounds to have their public playgrounds rebuilt. Exciting times, you might think, and money to be well spent. That was until the full extent of how much 'consultation' would be carried out was revealed. For more than six months surveys were carried out with local people to establish in which parts of the county the money should be spent because sadly there was not enough money to rebuild every playground in the area. The principle sounds good but essentially these surveys simply asked people across the town which playgrounds they felt were most in need of refurbishment. But the majority of children tend to use the playground nearest to their home with the occasional trip to a big, central park as a treat now and then. So if asked, aren't most people when asked simply going to choose the playground they use most often for the investment?

The simple answer is yes. And this is the way that this and virtually every other consultation I have ever seen works out. If you have money to spend people want it spent on their street, their park or their school. Members of the public don't have the time, or inclination, to visit every local facility they are being asked about to make an objective assessment and then make an appropriate decision. In mass consultations that ask this type of question, people understandably vote for what benefits them, most directly and most quickly.

It is because consultation has so often become about asking inane questions and getting the answers that anyone with half a brain would expect to get that the whole public involvement message is now so meaningless. Millions of pounds are spent each year by councils establishing what they already know, or least they would if they actually sat back and thought about it for a minute. The issues that they ask the public about are so obvious that it you have to wonder why they even bother asking the question.

Part of the problem with public consultation is basically the way that many council officers actually put things together. Take a recent consultation carried out in my own local authority. It was an online consultation that aimed to establish whether the council should invest in 'improving its online services' i.e. should it spend more money (presumably taken from another budget) to improve its website, develop e newsletters etc. Fair enough, you might think, it's important to invest in modern technology after all.

The first question (of about half a dozen or so) on the consultation was simply worded, 'Do you think we should improve our online services?' That was it. The public were expected to give a simple yes or no response to this question. No context. No explanation. No clarification about what this meant. No indication about how much things would actually cost. No clue as what other services might have to be cut. No information on where the money was to come from. Residents were expected to give a black or white response to something with little or no further information. How could this possibly result in a knowledgeable or informed response from the public?

One other observation is that the survey was done exclusively online. In other words, the only people asked for their opinion were those people who were already online savvy and presumably shopped and carried out other activities using their online access. Naturally, the opinions of this group are as important as anyone else's. But aren't almost all of this group by definition highly likely to be more supportive of improvements to online services, compared to someone, say, who is unable to access the internet, or simply who does not want to?

With so much of the community research that takes place little consideration is actually given to *who* is being asked *what*. The old analogy of turkeys being asked to vote for Christmas springs to mind . Ask a specific street if they want money spending on their street and don't be surprised if they say, "Yes please." Ask people if they want to open a young offenders facility next door and don't be surprised if they say, "No thanks." Similarly, if you want to spend money on new swings and slides at the a park at one end of the town, don't be shocked if people at the other end of town say they want the money instead because "That side of town get everything already and we don't get anything."

This is not to say that some consultation events are not meaningful to establish local opinions of course there are some. But unfortunately the whole consultation myth has been embraced so wholeheartedly that the actual reason for involving the public has been lost in a mad rush to ask pointless and idiotic questions that in real terms mean very little. The consultations take many forms, from postal surveys to public events at community centres, but the essence remains unchanged: let's give a vague impression of truly involving residents in decisions to show off how open and transparent we are being when actually all the important decisions are being made elsewhere and by other people.

Remember, of course, that all these consultations are not free. They all use staffing, resources, time, and effort. All in the name of openness. So who could argue that it is not money well invested? I heard the head of service from one local authority on a radio phone-in a couple of years ago. He was defending a decision to ban dog walkers from certain green areas of the district. Whether or not the decision was a correct one isn't the important thing in this case. The point about the interview that amazed me was the fact that the head of service defended every single line of reasoning against the decision by referring to the results of the consultation that had been carried out. Every counter argument was simply dismissed with, "Well the consultation we carried out showed overwhelming support for this move." That was it; that was the reasoning. Ultimately, I'm sure that was other reasons for the decisions but once things have been 'rubber stamped' by a public consultation that was the trump card to beat all other considerations. No more logic could be applied to counteract the decisions; the consultation work had been done and so no appeal was permitted.

However, one additional piece of information that made me smirk was that the consultation exercise to ban dog walkers from a few green spaces actually took three years to complete. Thirty-six long, arduous months to ask people a set of questions to establish where you can and cannot walk your dog. All paid for by you, the taxpayer. The Head of Service was incredibly proud of the period of time things had taken; for him it demonstrated thoroughness, hard work, and a commitment to involvement. I'd disagree. For me it demonstrates waste, a lack of decision-making skills and an inability to see when enough is enough.

The problem with the consultation as it is carried out currently is that it is done in complete isolation. Members of the public are not asked questions that actually mean anything because they are rarely given the full picture. What people are actually consulted on is often presented in such a simplistic way that it is utterly meaningless. You wouldn't make decisions in isolation within your personal finances but we still expect our electorate to make informed decisions on their local community in this way. For example, I wouldn't think of choosing the colour of my new Ferrari before I knew some basic things: do I have enough money to buy it; do I even want a Ferrari; do I even need a new car; can I afford to run it; is my job secure enough and well paid enough to justify buying one; can I park it somewhere; will anyone insure me on it; would the wife kill me if I came home with one; would the family savings be better spent on repairing the house roof? But councils feel that just because we've asked what colour the Ferrari should be then that justifies *all* elements of the decision.

I can see the quote from the elected officials now:

Official line: It's not our fault the old people's home is closed and that the streets are filthy. We consulted you over the building of the new £50 million town hall and there was overwhelming support for it. Unfortunately, these tough decisions have to be made.

Subtext: Well we held a competition with local school children to name the new building and lots of people agreed on the chosen name – that gives us carte blanche to do as wish around building a new town hall. The public has given us their support, after all.

Basically, I have a really fundamental discomfort with the concept of consultation. Ironically, my problem is that councils don't take consultation far enough. By this I don't mean that we should all be doing *more* consultation. That would simply make consultation overload into a consultation endemic. No, rather than this I mean that we should be doing less consultation (naturally) but making it more fundamental to the processes and systems of town halls up and down the land. In short, we should do fewer consultation exercises, but when we do carry them out we should use the information we get to make more important decisions.

Many of the public consultation events that you may attend yourself or read about in the local newspaper are arranged to discuss either quite specific things (merging of two schools; new road schemes) or relatively minor things (the colour of the swings in a new play area; the name of the new council building in the town centre). For me neither of these two groups of things is really what consultation should be about in the first place. This is simply picking stuff from a list, it is tokenism. It's giving people a list of things that have already been chosen, in order to spend a pre-determined amount that has already been decided upon by someone else. It's a step in the right direction but it's not enough.

My ambitious view is that consultation should be used to make much bigger decisions. Led by elected members, consultation exercises should consist of talking to the electorate about the issues that really matter – and in this case that means allocating council-wide budgets. Only when the public are actually involved in this fundamental decision-making process will consultation actually deliver on its big promises.

Let's be honest about things, people don't necessarily want 'choice' in their public service (or indeed involvement to a lesser degree). They want good schools, clean streets, and so on. The way consultation is set up now means that the focus is taken away from delivering these services and we simply end up talking about them. Really, how many different opinions can there be on how to sweep the streets? Community engagement must be about the big stuff – deciding how much each service should get. But no council in the land actually has the guts to let its communities decide on millions of pounds' worth of services. Far better to give a couple of resident committees a few hundred pounds every so often to make them think that they are actually able to get involved.

Take a recent community consultation exercise carried out in a small town in the South West. It involved giving a local neighbourhood (about a thousand residents) a budget of £25,000 to spend precisely as they wished on local projects. Local groups were invited to put forward projects that cost £5,000 each. These projects would all then be collated and local residents would be given information on each one and asked to vote on their favourite five. In this case twelve projects were put forward and a newsletter produced and sent to all the households with information on each one. The projects varied from new uniforms for the Boys' Brigade to free skips for all residents to get rid of their rubbish. The vote was then held (with an impressive 40% turnout) with the most popular five projects winning their £5,000 share of the money.

This project was held up as a fantastic example of community consultation at work. I'm more sceptical though. Great though it is to see the public being given money to spend I have a number of issues.

• Who chose how much money there was in the budget?

• Where did the money come from in the first place? i.e. what else might it have been spent on?

• Why £5,000 per project – why not give some of the projects a contribution, a smaller amount or a bigger amount if appropriate?

- Why did the whole project cost nearly £35,000 to deliver? That's £10,000 in additional costs.

- Does most popular project mean it is the most worthwhile?

- Would a proposal that gave every household £5 in cash win the public vote? And should it?

I know critics will accuse me of being pedantic over what was essentially a worthwhile project. But if this is how councils see consultations going then I still see it as little more than ticking a box to say that residents have been consulted. Particularly if the same council closes schools or reduces bus services to the very same community in the future.

Who's Fault?

"If they [the councillor] had been the CEO of a private company, he would find it easy to say, 'Let's do it and see.' But they cannot make a change without many stakeholders having their say. Indeed, consultation is the regime's preferred option for developing policy. The [councillor] can say that everyone has been consulted and... if anything goes wrong it is the consultees who will be to blame."

– John Seddon

As I have already touched on, the consultation game gives all those managers and councillors who seem unable or unwilling to make decisions a real get out jail free card. After all when these individuals are challenged over their inability to actually do anything what could be easier than to simply say; you are waiting for the results of the public consultation or that the project needs further public support before being rolled out further.

And this widespread consultation creates another of those unintended consequences. A situation where those paid to make decisions and to use their expertise to guide services are left to hide, procrastinate and keep their head firmly ensconced behind the parapet.

To a certain extent I can understand the problems that local authority managers face. I compare it to a situation I was in during my early days working within the evil private sector. At that time our company was going through some internal restructuring and as I result I ended up with two bosses for different aspects of my work. This might have been a workable situation but for the fact that the two managers didn't actually get on with each other and took every opportunity to wind each other up. Being piggy in the middle did little to help me do my work as I was told/asked to one thing one day only to be told the next day to ignore my previous instructions and to do something completely different.

Responding to the results of various consultation exercises is like council managers having two (or in some cases two hundred thousand) different bosses. Managing differing needs and priorities within services is the par for the course in local authority management. However, responding in a knee-jerk fashion to every public event, comment and complaint most certainly is not. In many councils every possible opportunity is taken to gauge what the public think; every piece of minutiae is examined, re-examined and reviewed to ensure that public opinion is respected at all costs. Even if this public opinion is misguided, ill-founded and downright wasteful to the silent majority.

A friend of mine works in the parks department of a neighbouring authority. One phone call he received from a member of the public involved a play area in a relatively modern housing estate. The play area was, as you might expect, placed in the middle of the estate as this meant that it was close to the households it was intended to serve. Fairly sensible really, as it would be a little stupid to have a local park three miles away from any housing. The phone call the officer in question went something like this:

Woman: I'd like to complain about the play park on Wisteria Lane.

Officer: Really madam, what's the problem?

Woman: Well the thing is, it's attracting children.

Officer: Er... right, OK. Well I believe that's what it is meant to do. Are they causing a disturbance? Is it late at night or anything?

Woman: Not really. It's just that when I'm in my garden I can hear them playing. I wasn't really expecting that when I moved here, and I don't really like the noise they make.

Officer: OK, so how can we help?

Woman: I was hoping you could move the play area.

Believe it or not this conversation started a whole raft of meetings, councillor surgeries and letter drops to see what the neighbours thought of the local play area. All this work carried out to ensure that we delivered against what the public wanted. Nothing wrong with the principle, of course, but as always with these types of consultations it tends to be the usual suspects, the local 'characters' who come out to make their feelings known. The vast majority as always remain quiet and unheard. In this case you won't be surprised to learn that the park wasn't moved, but the fact that so much time and effort had to be wasted to establish what good old-fashioned common sense would have told you typifies the attitude of many local councils that no decision can actually be made (and fought for if necessary) without *everyone's* opinion being sought.

And that's the point. The more people you ask the more different opinions you get. The more opinions you get the less clear the picture often becomes. Particularly when there is rarely anyone in authority who can actually sort out what all this feedback from the public means, what weight it should carry, what other factors are involved and so ultimately what the 'right' decision is. In short, if councils continue to ask all their bosses about everything how will anything ever actually get done?

This proliferation of opinions is only part of the story. The difficulty these opinions cause only goes part of the way to really explain the procrastination and indecision that results. Managers in local authorities must once again take their fair share of the blame. Unpopular though it may seem to be, council officers must take the opportunity to use their brains and experience to sort out the wheat from the chaff and that simply does not happen enough. All too often officers take the opportunity to avoid actually doing any work under the pretence of consultation and public involvement. But then I suppose it saves them the troublesome requirements of making a decision.

No council officer or elected member will ever take it upon themselves to say to pressure groups, user forums or anyone else that while their opinions are valid, ultimately the decision will be made based on *all* the available evidence as to whether the sewerage works (or young offenders home etc.) will be located at X or Y. Tough decisions are just that, tough; and the path of least resistance is not always the right one although it is invariably the one taken. But the public sector being what it is woe betide any individual or department who actually decides something on behalf of the community. To say, "In my experience, and taking all factors into account, I believe that..." is no longer acceptable in any circumstances. Sure, some decisions are unpopular, some decisions are wrong, but these are not reasons never to make another decision ever again.

To look at the strength of local consultation power I had a quick look through the websites of a variety of local newspapers a few years ago. The list below gives a flavour of just some of the public campaigns that headlined in these papers up and down the country against the actions of a local council and the plans they have consulted on. I have not been selective here. Every local newspaper I looked at had at least one example from the previous couple of months:

Brighton – Library/Community Hub

Croydon – Coulsden Pay and Display Plans

Dorset – Pavilion Protest

Kent – Birchington Arcade

Leicestershire – Melton Phone Mast

Malvern – Hagley Hall office development

Oxfordshire – Watlington Church Hall closure

Pembrokeshire – Local school closure

Ramsgate – Protest at art cafe late night hours ban

I highlight these examples not to suggest that any single one of them is anything less than worthy but simply to show that for every decision made somebody somewhere is almost certainly bound to be against it for one reason or another.

Basically, giving everybody everywhere the right to reply might create a certain element of transparency but the flipside means that every decision becomes contentious and people actually feel more ignored than before. Not because – as some people feel – that consultation is there to simply rubber stamp a decision that has already been made, but because those who are consulted have their expectations raised too high. They are led to believe that it is their opinions and these alone that will decide things. But we all know that life is about compromises and that as grown-ups we sometimes don't our own way.

Only by having mature sensible discussions about different alternatives and options will consultation become about real involvement rather than simply asking opinions and being forced to ignore the wishes of somebody somewhere. The opportunity exists to involve people in this way but as councils we too often treat the public like children and don't give people all the facts. We need to be honest and upfront enough to say to people that some of them might not get their own way. This isn't the same as ignoring them.

While I concede I am critical of councils I refuse to believe that every decision they make is wrong. But reading about these campaigns you would believe that this is the case. We seem to miss the fact that if 10% of people sign a petition then 90% of people didn't have the interest, passion or interest in what was going on. This isn't being defeatist, it is being practical. Sometimes, just sometimes, people have to accept that they won't get their way.

Officers and councillors do not cover themselves in

glory when they lead these public consultation events. Local authority representatives have a duty to be open and honest with residents. But far too often we speak to residents from a pre-prepared script and continually toe the official line. We make excuses, try to justify unreasonable stances and are generally just overly defensive. Anything we can do to avoid actually coming across as a sensible human being with a willingness to debate and share information.

Of course there is a fine line to tread when officers and councillors are in public arenas. Officers shouldn't just sit and criticise the local authority; that is unnecessary and unproductive – if somewhat tempting. But officers do need to be forthcoming enough so that it is actually worth residents coming along.

The Way Forward

"Nothing will ever be attempted if all possible objections must first be overcome."

– Samuel Johnson

The solution is very much the same as we have seen throughout the whole of this book. A simple and uncomplicated solution that will be incredibly hard to actually make stick. Do less consultation on things that people don't want to know about, carry out less box ticking and actually *involve* the local electorate in decisions.

I have been very critical of the way that too many councils have knee-jerk reactions to what they perceive as public opinion and this is of course not to dismiss involvement from local people all together. Far from it. Instead councils must have the guts to actually make decisions on their own; this does not mean riding roughshod over local campaign groups and petitions, but rather looking at things more widely.

To say that the public has no say in things currently is simply not right. In many cases the public has too much say. Services are too often guilty of not being able to say no to 'left field' demands and opinions, to rightly dismiss the very vocal and very small minorities – those nutters who frankly do little more than waste time and resources for local authority staff.

All this sounds as though I have a downer on the public's right to campaign and express opinions. Nothing could be further from the truth. I am a huge advocate of community involvement. But the point is that right now we mess about with it. Community involvement means that sometimes 'the public' doesn't get what it wants. If consultation was better handled and expectations weren't raised so ridiculously high then the majority of people would be understanding enough to accept decisions.

I would propose that rather than consultation being limited to picking the colour of the bike racks at the new secondary school residents should be able to be consulted on bigger issues – like whether we need the school in the first place if it means the care home down the road closes. And this resident involvement primarily hinges on changing the role of elected councillors. As we have seen there are some huge limitations to the way that your local ward councillor operates. But if the role of these councillors was genuinely to represent the people who voted them in then this would be a step in the right direction.

To do this is simple and again involves councillors changing their priorities and moving towards independence rather than staying engrained in party politics. If councillors are there to represent a particular ward then that is what they must do. They must work very, very hard to establish what the few thousand people in their ward actually want in the big areas such as annual budget setting and capital investment programmes. The politicians then simply must vote on what they have been told by their electorate, not on what party HQ and their muckers in the town hall tell them to.

Despite my contempt for local politicians, if we can move away from the attitude that councillors have been voted in on a left- or right-wing mandate and move them onto truly representing the people's opinions then consultation becomes, whilst perhaps not completely redundant, certainly less of a problem. Consultation on everything is no longer as necessary because on the big stuff (where it really matters) a greater number of people have had their say in the first place.

Ultimately we just need a more grown-up way of working with public opinion. There is an old adage that you can't please all the people all the time. It is so true, but currently we seem to please virtually none of the people most of the time. While I don't advocate taking our bat and ball home by saying to ourselves well why bother trying then I think we (councils as well as public) need to accept that if someone is asked for their opinion it is their right to be heard. However, it is not their right to get their own way.

9. Up a Bit, Down a Bit, Left a Bit... FIRE!

"To be sure of hitting the target, shoot first, and call whatever you hit the target."

– Ashleigh Brilliant

Targets have been part of many people's day to day work life at for decades. Salesmen, for example, have their own set of individual targets to hit, with their salaries often based on hitting a certain level of sales. Other targets are more organisationally focused, such as supermarkets aiming to increase their market share or shops aiming to improve their stock turnover. Targets then, are an everyday reality for thousands of people in the private sector.

Companies may use targets to motivate individuals to increase productivity, to help set the direction for the future or to enable the management team to decide on priorities and allocate resources accordingly. So you won't be surprised to learn that the local authority paymasters in Whitehall have seen this idea of using targets to deliver improvements and have subsequently jumped on the bandwagon.

Setting targets and 'measuring things' has been embraced wholeheartedly by every single town hall as they aim to standardize services up and down the country and demonstrate just how fantastic they are at delivering services for their local electorate. In short, the targets and measurement approach helps everyone involved to see that the levels of anti-social behaviour are reducing in Cornwall at comparable rates to those in Carlisle. Or that children in one school in Croydon are performing to the same standard as ones on the other side of town.

The principle for these targets remains the same whether councils are looking at the cleanliness of streets, the air quality in a town centre, or the length of time people have to wait for a house. They are trying to measure specific performance in order to promote improvement and to allow different services to be compared either within one council or between different councils.

The Targets Culture

"In the face of evidence showing targets produce perverse consequences people who believe in targets simply assume they need to refine the targets or identify the 'bad apples' who prevent them from working."

– John Seddon

So what is so wrong with measuring things and using this as a basis for improving public service? Surely this is the one of the best things that can be done in order to drag councils kicking and screaming into the real world and to help provide better services for its residents.

The use of targets in local government is an extension of the notion that 'what gets measured gets managed, and what doesn't get measured does not get managed'. This idea is one that commentators have been discussing for many years without really coming to any definite consensus. However, many of them do agree that measurements need to be appropriate and balanced, that they should not become the sole focus of people's work and that targets should be used as a means rather than an end in themselves.

But it is exactly these traps that councils fall into. One of the main problems of using targets as we do in councils is the culture that they seem to induce amongst the staff. Essentially targets are seen as the *raison d'être* above all else. Targets become the reason for getting up in the morning and if this means that common sense (which obviously isn't that common) and customer service fly out of the window then so be it.

In all of the services I have worked we have had a number of different targets to hit – both nationally determined ones and locally created ones. Managers in every case have moved resources around their department to ensure that these targets are hit irrespective of the effect on other services and even whether the targets should be being hit in the first place.

Let me give an example of what I mean. In my early days working in this quagmire of bureaucracy, councils were required to make assessments of their services against the nationally set Best Value Performance Indicators which are now defunct (although the principles remain). There were nearly 1200 different measures that councils had to pick their way through and I was lucky enough to be involved in the assessment of just a few of these.

I forget what the names and numbers of these measurements were but effectively they were put in place to assess how clean the streets, parks and town centres of each and every authority in the country were against a national benchmark. All 400-odd authorities were given a simple-to-use, fifty-page guidance manual that outlined the methodology, sample size, and so on. Basically the target required an 'independent' team from our council to spend two full weeks of every year visiting around two hundred randomly selected locations in the town to count the number of pieces of litter in a ten metre sample size. Yes, that's right, to assess the quality of our street cleaning we had two staff counting bits of litter in the street for two weeks. A fortnight later our department had a range of numbers that we were able to report to various managers, directors and councillors to show how fantastic we were.

So it sounds a bit like overkill but is it that bad? Well this is only the start; our managers felt that the percentage figure that we would receive at the end of this charade was so important that we should give ourselves every opportunity to get the best score possible. This wasn't cheating, you understand, heaven forbid. No, it was simply making sure that our department received the score that it deserved. Nothing more and nothing less.

We were quite lucky really as the team who were carrying out the assessment were actually part of the same service as us. This meant that there was a certain amount of control that our service manager had over them, to say the least. This led us to a happy compromise to ensure a fair assessment was carried out and that we received the correct score. The inspection team simply told us where and when they would be inspecting. This meant we could arrange for half a dozen of our street cleaning crews to stop what they should have been doing (looking after the electorate) and get them to pay a visit to the inspection area half an hour before the inspectors arrived. Easy really!

The result was a score that our street cleaning team were happy with and warm feeling of satisfaction that the assessment team had done their job according to the specification they had been given. Sadly, however, it meant that the score wasn't actually a reflection of what the executives and Whitehall boffins wanted it to be; it didn't give a true picture of reality and most worryingly of all it meant that services were distorted and changed in order to solely hit some arbitrary target.

This is just one example of the targets culture and why it just doesn't seem to hit the mark. Proponents of the target based approach would argue that this is simply a case of one bad manager spoiling things for everyone else. This just isn't true. Very few targets are actually measured fairly by any definition of the word. Some managers explicitly fiddle the numbers by just writing the number that they want in the appropriate column. After all, who can actually check their accuracy? Other managers like the one above just bring enough pressure to bear so that the target is hit by simply ensuring the measure is taken on a 'good day'.

The positive thing about these managers at least is that they don't necessarily waste huge amounts of time and resources pandering to the target hunters. They simply do enough to keep out of trouble for not completing the forms and in some cases they move small amounts of resources on the appropriate day.

The majority of managers are not as pragmatic as this though. They seem to have accepted that targets are the Holy Grail of service improvements. These managers literally move heaven and earth to ensure that the figure achieved at the end of the year is on target. This group might include the head teacher who is required to get as many children as possible gaining a C grade or above in their GCSEs. The head teacher might put intensive resources into getting children on course for a 'D' up to the magic 'C' grade. This means extra lessons for those specific children and coaching in preparation for the exam – not in itself a bad thing, of course. Meanwhile those on course for an 'F' are given negligible support to get them up to an 'E' because in terms of hitting targets, where's the benefit? Similarly, they are no incentives to get the 'B' students up to an 'A', so why give them any extra help?

Similarly, this is the manager who is part of the local authority wide drive to ensure as few pupils as possible are excluded from school. The result is that behaviour that would have previously result in a child being permanently excluded from school (serious wounding of a teacher or something) will now result in alternatives being put in place – counselling, anger management, armed guards in every classroom etc.

This is also the manager who has been given a target of turning round social care assessments in a specific number of days. The manager believes the target is unrealistic as these assessments can take weeks, so all they have to do is shift the focus of the service. Gone is the emphasis on actually providing the much-needed support for the elderly, giving them nursing care etc. as this is replaced with more resources being spent on carrying out the assessments within the timescales required. The emphasis on making the assessments of a high quality also disappears to be replaced with an overriding requirement simply to carry them out quickly, whether they are accurate or not becomes of secondary importance. Anything to make sure the target is hit.

This is the targets culture at its ugliest as people get treated like numbers and priorities become all about the targets rather than all about the service users and making the *right* decision. This culture isn't about a few naughty boys and girls misunderstanding the targets or doing things that will make them look good. This is about creating systems and approaches that breed contempt for the quality of services that need to be provided and an overzealous drive to hitting a magic number.

So we end up in a position where people are driven to achieve the targets no matter how pointless or inappropriate they actually are. On top of that, though, yet another cottage industry is created where measuring becomes the end rather than the means. Like many of the cottage industries that we have seen the measurement of targets needs to have a surprisingly large infrastructure surrounding it. Some councils need a Performance Management Unit, the associated staff, training programmes and ubiquitous expensive software system in order to manage the newly collected information.

These Performance Management Units are often there to simply collect information and ask questions of managers. These questions aren't constructive ones about how the service is going, are staff performing well but rather things like, "Dave, it's the twenty-eighth of the month, you haven't completed section three of the Performance Management System; indicator seven hasn't been flagged up as complete for this month – it needs completing because otherwise it looks like we haven't done anything when the report is printed off."

How did we get to this position? A manager who coordinates thirty staff, an annual budget of nearly £2 million, and whose service looks after the welfare of 100,000 people getting told by an administrator that it appears they aren't doing anything, not because the department is shambles or they've had hundreds of complaints (although they may well have done) but because the appropriate column on a computer system hasn't had the right number put in it.

The main reason for this fixation on hitting targets above all else is that this is where the funding comes from. Only by hitting targets can any council hope to continue to receive government grants; only by hitting targets can they attract funding for pilot programmes and only by hitting targets can they hope to attract money from other funding sources. Wouldn't you have a fixation on targets with everything else (like keeping residents happy) coming a distant second?

But if these targets lead to service improvements, what

is wrong with this fixation? Surely that's what we are looking for. But that is the key point. Rarely, if ever, do these targets actually make services better, not because they are they are wrongly specified (although plenty are) but because the whole notion of hitting targets in this culture is flawed. Staff think numbers first and think about what they *really* mean second. Services don't actually improve, the numbers just get better, the spin improves, and everyone involved can evade responsibility by pointing at graphs and charts.

One amusing effect of the targets culture in the town hall is 'target envy'. Just like having your own strategy or partnership, having a target within local government circles means that 'you've arrived'. Only important things after all could possibly have targets so if you don't have one, you and your department might as well not exist.

So while many managers and staff would decry (often in public) the fact that targets are ruining the fabric of local government, these very same people actually go on to create more of their own made-up targets. They go for accreditation from national governing bodies, look for awards from various organisations that demand x, y and z figures are achieved, or alternatively just set their own random figures to hit by next year and then report back to the councillors and Chief Executive how well they are hitting their own 'local service outcome based targets'. Anything that makes the manager and their department stand out when councillors and senior directors have their meetings. So there ends up being two camps in councils: those who have targets and complain about having to hit them, and the other group who protest and worry that they are not included on the 'measurement list'.

Management by Numbers (Part 1)

"A kid in her form asked the head for two weeks' holiday during term time and he has granted them permission. That's because the 'permission' is a charade anyway; if he says 'no' they'll go anyway and it will spoil our figures under the new government initiative to reduce unauthorised absences. This is another tremendous example of how things can be easily improved by totting up numbers in different columns."

– Frank Chalk

One of the main advantages for staff working in the town halls is that using targets and these arbitrarily allocated measurements is that it takes management down to its most simple denominator: numbers. For councillors, directors and all managers, the idea of being able to manage the incredibly complex world of an organisation that looks after adult social care, street cleaning and education by simply looking at a number must sound incredibly appealing. And by wholeheartedly adopting the targets culture managers are able to reduce services to a series of numbers in a report.

Targets then become an easy (if completely flawed) way for senior staff to assess if things are going well in their council. What is easier to understand than a 1% shortfall in one area, or a red flag to indicate a problem in another? What's harder to understand is how a service actually runs, what residents really want and how the complex business of staff motivation and service delivery interact.

Everyone involved in the targets game has a strange obsession with numbers and end up quoting them endlessly often completely out of context. Indeed they have become so engrained in local government circles that not a day goes by without someone quoting a random statistic at you to back up their case for a fantastic improvement or catastrophic deterioration in standards.

One example comes from my colleagues who work in the county Safer Neighbourhoods Team. Basically they are a council unit who work closely with the local police to reduce crime and raise resident awareness about crime prevention. Yet another worthy cause for us to be involved in. But just one of many that ties itself up in knots with pointless and misleading targets.

I worked with one officer who arranged regular meetings with local neighbourhood watch groups, police officers, and residents to discuss the local crime picture and how the community felt that they wanted services to address problems. Again you will notice here another example of the high visibility service delivery that councils and the police seem so keen on.

The highlight of the meetings each month for me was the crime figures update. My colleague would step in at this time to reveal the monthly figures for how many old ladies had been mugged in the area over the last four weeks, how many cars had been stolen and so on.

All sounds good, doesn't it? That is until the officer in question decides to compare these figures with the local crime targets. One particular monologue went something like this:

"Well everyone we've had a fantastic September for criminal damage. We've had only sixteen reported incidents in the month with just two more days to go before October. Our locally agreed target was twenty so that means that we are allowed another three incidents in the next two days and we will still be better than our target."

I can't quite put my finger on it but something is very wrong somewhere. The officer in question might have phrased their statement badly, and of course we must allow for this, but somehow this was just a reflection of the overriding sense that if we manage all services according to strict number and targets then all will be rosy in the garden.

The officer in question seemed to have no real sense of what these numbers actually meant. Or at least the context in which they existed anyway. Every number quoted was, in fact, a person. Saying that even if we have three more people affected by crime over the weekend then that's still OK because the numbers will be on target sadly completely misses this point. And that is the problem with the management by numbers brigade – they can't see beyond the figures or even begin to comprehend that actually there are indeed 'lies, damn lies, and statistics'.

It is important here that we don't completely dismiss the use of numbers, of course. However, context is the key thing here. Targets in themselves are not a bad thing but people's reliance on them and attitude towards their application is most certainly less than helpful.

The management by numbers approach allows lots of pretty graphs, charts and tables to appear in the performance management systems that operate in councils. Nothing shows how wonderfully well a council service is being run as well as an elegantly constructed table of numbers. But these aids to management are a double-edged sword.

While they allow plenty of publicity to be created, fundamentally they make people think they understand a service when in reality they may have no idea whatsoever how the service and people in question really operate. And this approach of managing by numbers becomes incredibly dangerous as those people who manage the targets themselves become the all-powerful and supposedly all-knowing ones. They become the people who decide on priorities, on where the money needs to be spent and so on. All with little more knowledge then the computer printout they've received on which services are doing what.

But this is the way that management runs in your council. Success is not based on whether the residents are happy with how clean the streets are or on whether old Mrs Jones is given all the support and advice she needs to live an independent life in her own house. No. Success is managed on the number of green flags a manager gets on their monthly returns; failure is assessed as the number of red flags they get.

This targets approach gives (a pretty blunt) measurement in some sectors such as sales where it is much more about the numbers. In the world of large organisations these numbers simply oversimplify the complexities and remove any notion of meaning. Let's pick up on the example of the street cleaning assessments that we saw earlier.

The manager in question was set a target of let's say 80% of local streets to hit the national standard for cleanliness. In year one the level is at 75%, year two 78% and in year three the 80% target is hit. All the directors notice the figures and are suitably impressed by the ongoing improvement. But should they be?

The answer is a resounding 'almost certainly not'. We have already seen earlier how the measurement process can be so easily massaged. But to say this is the only problem is not quite true. The managers in street cleaning tell me that measuring street cleanliness is fundamentally flawed simply because of all the variables involved. (Sorry to bore you with this but my colleagues bored me so it's only fair that I pass it on.) Essentially, there are many things that affect the cleanliness of a given street on any one day:

- Wind – a windy day blows litter around, meaning that no one knows where it will settle. In short, one gust of wind can make street cleaned two minutes earlier look like a bomb site.

- Rain – people drop litter. If it's raining there are fewer people out on the streets and so this means less litter.

- Time of day – school leaving times, after the pubs are shut etc. When lots of people walk by a certain place there is more litter; measure just before and you're onto a winner.

- Bin day – wheelie bins and recycling boxes on the street for collection mean more litter; no bins means less litter in that street.

So if you assess the streets on a wet day when the wind has just blown all the litter away at a time before school lunchtime and you get a fantastic result; do it on a day when the opposite is true and the result is disastrous. Would you want to manage a multi-million pound service based on the numbers you are given as a result of this 'fair and independent measure'?

Street cleaning is just one simplistic example but every service that is affected by a complexity of figures. Safer Neighbourhoods and a one-man, one-off crime wave that dents their figures; a small school intake affected by one or two geniuses who by some accident of numbers went into the same school year. The list goes on where figures are affected by the randomness of life.

And this word 'random' is perhaps the key one here. Any mathematician will tell you that in a series of numbers you are going to have a natural variation. Even if the numbers are being influenced in some way – as us lot in the council think we are doing – then there is still a natural variance amongst anything. Any researcher worth their salt will tell you that. Whether it is the squirrel population in a forest or the number of vulnerable adults being taken in to sheltered accommodation the world is a chaotic place and there will be fluctuations in any series of numbers. For the sample size that most councils use a margin of error of around 4-5% is not unreasonable. Suddenly that three percent improvement in street cleanliness seems less a bit less impressive.

Because people in local authorities are so geared up towards targets their understanding of these fluctuations seems to fly out of the window. The Street Cleaning Manager earlier who sees an increase in the numbers does not temper his confidence in them by saying that actually the numbers were affected by the closure of the local chip shop. Nor does he see that, actually, the improvements are so small that they could just be part of the natural trend of numbers and that next year even without doing anything they might go up again, or that he might double his efforts and the numbers actually stay about the same.

I'm the first to admit that if the numbers show a dramatic improvement and continue to do so for several years then clearly something is affecting them, but as we have seen this might not exactly mean that things are genuinely getting better. But if the numbers show that things are actually getting worse (despite everyone's best efforts) then that is the point that the excuses are wheeled out.

- "Well actually the target is an unfair measure of performance in this case."

- "It has been an exceptional year in many ways so the failure to hit this target is nothing more than a small glitch."

- "Many unforeseen events this year have had an effect on hitting this year's targets; we do not expect these to occur again and as such will be back on target very soon."

Human nature being what it is, and most local authority managers being (at least partly) human, the excuses come out for failures as shown above and everyone wants to take the credit when targets are supposedly exceeded. Everyone hates the targets if they are not hitting them, and love them if they are.

These numbers come to mean everything. Hitting 75% of something equates to a heralded success; 60% means you're rubbish and should give up the day job. Few people see the targets as arbitrary numbers though and actually treat them with undue reverence and seriousness. Who is to say that 75% is good and 60% is not. Maybe 100% is the only acceptable number and everything else actually represents failure for the public.

But then targets don't really work like that; those who assess them rarely understand the complexities of service delivery and end up just making an educated guess about what the target should be. What could be easier than to measure what the level is now and then just increase it by 2% without necessarily understanding whether that figure is reasonable, achievable, challenging or even desirable.

Unintended Consequences

"Surely there comes a time when counting the cost and paying the price aren't things to think about any more. All that matters is value – the ultimate value of what one does."

– James Hilton

One of the most worrying results of the targets culture is the gradual erosion of any kind of honesty and frankness about services. Because of the comparisons that are made between councils regionally and nationally using these targets and figures everyone involved is keen to look good by getting themselves to the top of the tree. Remember this doesn't mean that the council at the top of the league table has the best services. They just have the best numbers.

But in order to get the best numbers you need to play the game and this is where fair dealing flies out of the window. If you're a manager of any particular council service and you know that your department is not great but that you are working damn hard to make things better are you going to be brave enough to put your head above the parapet and honestly let it be known that you are performing at 20% but improving? Especially when the neighbouring council are claiming to be at 80%. Not a chance really because you're going to look stupid in front of everyone, the councillors will lose votes and the service will look shabby. No far easier in this case to join them rather than beat them.

The targets culture also throws up a range of perverse situations that come about as managers are forced to make ridiculous decisions just in order to hit targets. In one school I visited a couple of years ago as I walked into the reception area I was greeted by ripped and tatty carpets, doors barely clinging on to their hinges, flaking paint and a general stench of damp. It was like a step back into the Great Depression. I was then shown into a few classrooms to have a look round and the general condition of these rooms was equally shabby. Clearly the school was desperately short of money to carry out even the most basic refurbishment and repairs. However, I could hardly fail to notice that each classroom also had brand new, state of the art, electronic smart boards at a couple of thousand pounds each. The contrast between these and the rest of the building was glaring.

The head of the school was relatively new and passionate about improving the condition of the school for its pupils. Money had been awarded to the school by the relevant local authority but rather than being given the opportunity to spend this money on what was needed for the school it had been given solely to be spent on SMART boards to ensure that the IT targets were hit locally. To make sure that 100% of schools have SMART board technology by the end of the year. No flexibility, no compromise. Spend it on IT or don't get the money.

I'm not questioning the value of IT equipment in schools here. However, I do question the sense in spending upwards of £40,000 in one school on SMART boards to be put up in draughty, cold, bleak, damp classrooms. Does that really create an environment conducive to learning? Does it provide the best possible start for those children or does it simply keep the bean counters happy back at base? It might or might not but it would be nice for the decisions to be made for the right reasons.

But decisions are rarely made for the right reasons. Even if a good decision is made it is usually by chance rather than design. Targets and spurious numbers pervade so many aspects of the work done by councils that the overall direction and understanding of what is actually important disappears off the radar. Councils are given targets from above by Whitehall, Chief Executives and councillors but then also set huge stall by their various consultations to determine what local people want from their town hall officers. Unfortunately with so much 'direction' this does little more than create more and more opportunity for conflict.

So what happens when targets and local consultations are in conflict and disagree on what's important? Who wins the battle for what's important, the top brass and their targets or the lowly citizens? The targets and the bureaucracy win every time, of course. In other words, councils respond to the needs of local people unless of course those needs are different from 'our' direction in which case we just default to hitting the targets.

I recall being interviewed for one job with my current council by a panel of managers along with representatives from HR and local organisations. One of the questions that they asked me was exactly along these lines. They asked me to imagine a situation where senior management direction/targets were in direct conflict with what citizens wanted. Which side should be given the priority? I waffled on about compromise, understanding both sides of the argument etc. for a minute or so and finally came to my coup de grace. Basically, I said, wherever possible priority should be given to the local situation and what local people have asked for. Not in every case, naturally, but more weight should be given to them in any decision-making process; ultimately, this might still mean that the top-down targets would still 'win' but that due consideration had been given to residents.

So as interview questions go I thought I'd done OK, answering on the hoof but at least explaining that as a local authority we were there to serve the community in the area. Sadly, the panel did not appear to share my enthusiasm for people power. I've answered questions badly in interviews before and the interviewers have politely nodded and quickly moved on in an act of sympathy. In this case, however, the panel just looked at me in a puzzled way. They looked at each other. Back at me and seemed on the verge of asking me what the hell I was talking about and how on earth any human being could possibly answer the question like this. In fairness they stopped short of this and simply shook their heads disapprovingly and moved on to the next question safe in the knowledge that this particular candidate would get nowhere near being offered the job.

Councils are given funding based on how deprived their particular area is: the more people on benefits, or in poor health or without an education, the more money the council gets. While the logic is sound as these are the areas that by definition need more support from councils it does create a strange culture. The worse an area is, the more money it gets. This creates a situation for the council and its officer where if they make improvements it means losing money (and potentially jobs as a result). It is naturally difficult to know what to really do for the best. Do a good job by making improvements and effectively you are being punished. Alternatively do an adequate (or even a bad) job and things stay pretty much the same for all involved and the money continues to pour in.

So you might say change the system so that improvements are rewarded. That's already been tried and it just means the numbers get fiddled, systems get changed and priorities shifted to suit whatever particular target needs to be hit that week. Lasting changes are never, ever made because the targets shift continuously. This means that the service suffers because of the emphasis on keeping the money coming in by hitting the numbers no matter what they are, what they mean or indeed where the money comes from.

An Inspector Calls

"The great day arrives. We have spent weeks in our attempt to pull the wool over the eyes of the Ofsted Inspection Team. All sorts of policies and action plans are in place, whether or not they work or even have any meaning. Bay trees appear outside and everything is painted and cleaned. In short, we have done everything except address any of our real problems."

– Frank Chalk

Of course with so many targets and the associated guidance and rules there is naturally a requirement for inspections to take place on a regular basis. You are probably well familiar with the Ofsted inspections wonderfully described by Frank Chalk above. Essentially, every school has to be inspected by government officials every couple of years or so to make sure that the children aren't being taught anything useful and that the teachers are happy with the size of their staff room.

The good news is that inspections aren't limited to schools. Every council also gets their own version of these inspections. But the principle of all of these inspections remains the same. To make sure that councils are doing a good job. No, don't laugh, it's true. The boffins at Whitehall arrange for a team of two or three 'experts' to visit each and every town hall in the land to see what is being done and how well.

The first thing to point out at this stage is that these inspections are not surprise visits carried out by mystery shoppers or by inspectors just 'calling in' on the way past. That would just be a little too unfair on those involved. So instead each council gets plenty of warning before the inspectors call. Usually this warning is at least a few weeks to allow managers plenty of time to prepare their scripts.

There is rumour that the queen thinks that the whole world smells of paint. This is of course because everywhere that she visits is aware she is coming and so there is always a mad rush to ensure that everywhere she sees is cleaned, polished and freshly painted. And it is this mad rush that is the best analogy I can find for the reaction town halls have for the news that a national inspection is looming. These inspections are different from the internally led assessments that I touched upon earlier only in scale and the fact that the people coming need slightly thicker and better quality wool to be pulled over their eyes.

In most of the authorities I have worked at the impending inspection is preceded by a number of key steps:

- Information to all staff – usually a memo or an email, this prepares the ground nicely scaring the crap out of those who care about the visit and letting everyone know that the brown, smelly stuff is about to hit the plastic whirly thing.

- Staff briefing – this colloquialism basically means that managers are able to pass on the pre-arranged script to their staff, including lists of do and don'ts ('don't mention the war,' that kind of thing). It also means that staff holidays can be arranged to hide the less photogenic or inspection-friendly staff.

- Paperwork review – paperwork is very important to inspectors so managers take this four minute warning as the ideal opportunity to just double check that they have everything documented as they should. Of course everything is already in place but it doesn't do anyone any harm to work long into the night catching up.

- Spit and polish – inspectors don't really care what the town hall looks or smells like but there's no harm in repainting the doors and landings; getting some new blinds for the office where they'll be based; buying in the posh biscuits and paper doilies and putting on the percolator to give the whole place that beautiful, freshly-brewed coffee smell. There might be a few extra points in that after all.

I fibbed about the biscuits but the rest is pretty much true. Again, human nature, you'll say. Everyone prepares at the last minute for an exam or whatever. But this goes deeper than that – these are *your* services. They should be ready for an inspection at all times.

But the nature of these inspections is probably the key point of concern here. If these inspections were the mystery shopper type approach, or were purely there to look at how the public perceived services or how effective the 'meals on wheels' service was than yes giving councils notice of inspections is ludicrous. Sadly inspections do not seem to have these things in mind when they visit. Inspections instead focus on making sure that all the paperwork is in order.

Basically the boffins come to inspect the myriad of strategies that sit on shelves in the town hall. They start with a conversation with the CEO and they fill in the inspection team on what a wonderful two years the council has had writing all the strategies, forming lots of partnerships and delivering well… er… not very much but how everything is going wonderfully well anyway.

The inspectors then spend the next couple of days trying to digest the vast pile of paperwork that the senior officers of the council dump in front of them. Organisational charts, strategies, policies, action plans, meeting notes, staff appraisals and press cuttings are all there to be read, poured over and discussed with the senior management team. All these glossy documents covered earlier then serve a purpose at last. They show just how busy and effective your council is working on your behalf to the central government team of experts.

So the next step you would hope would be for the inspectors to use the following few days (or indeed weeks) to visit the local electorate, talk to the front line staff and sample some of the services for themselves. This would at least give them an overview of how good or bad things really are. Unfortunately the time inspectors spend in each local authority is so limited that once they have finished looking through the plans and talking to senior (and some middle) management their visit is over.

So these independent inspectors spend little more than

a few days in each council. They look through paperwork that has been written, prepared, edited and censored by senior management to make damn sure it says all the right things for the boffins. Presentations are prepared and delivered to the inspection team to back up all the things that are said in the documents. Finally, a small number of stooges are presented to the inspectors to read their prepared scripts. Sorry, I mean to answer the inspector's tough and probing questions.

All in all then a complete charade from start to finish. It's all little more than a game. Everyone knows the script; everyone knows all the moves and everyone sticks rigidly to their pre-agreed part. The inspectors come along, go through motions and leave in readiness for writing their reports.

Those councils who receive glowing reports naturally bask in the glory ignoring the fact that although services *might* be good, in reality they just had the paperwork in good order and fell lucky on inspection day. Senior managers and councillors would never let the truth stand in the way of good press though.

On the other hand those councils who get disappointing or even downright bad reports immediately wheel out the excuses as we have seen above along with the age-old "This inspection report is from some time ago and we have already made significant improvements to our services." So while the good scores get crowed about by all involved, the low scores get largely ignored and appealed against.

Surely if the inspection process is to mean anything then there simply can't be any room for all this wriggling and excuses. If we genuinely had confidence in the whole inspection process then a bad report should mean that council management is hauled over the coals. Sadly everyone in the system knows that the inspection process is not thorough or robust enough for the findings to actually mean anything and so they don't actually carry any teeth. The result is a wish-washy system that only allows good results for councils or excuses.

Ultimately this means that no one benefits; we don't have a clear picture of how councils are really performing, time is wasted as councils use resources just becoming 'inspection ready' and the powers that be continue patting themselves on the back for a wonderful system of categorising and classifying councils for the benefit of every resident. But this is far better than actually carrying out proper inspections; god alone knows what kind of chaos and mismanagement they would discover.

The Way Forward

"The art of being wise is knowing what to overlook."

– William James

Various governments and council hierarchies have tried over the last few years to change this target culture. Sadly this has not quite had the impact that many of us might hope. Rather than have a root and branch review of the whole targets approach the easiest thing for everyone involved has been to just tinker with things. Admittedly the tinkering has seen the number of targets used nationally dramatically reduce and inspections become better or removed altogether but this is not the same as changing the culture. Especially when most have simply been replaced by new self-set targets that councils have put in place because they like the idea of measuring stuff so much and have leapt headlong onto the targets bandwagon.

Instead of this tweaking, targets need throwing forcefully out of the window. They are cumbersome and poor at really seeing whether councils are any good simply because the minute you start to measure something it improves simply through the action of measuring it. I call it the 'oh bugger someone's watching we better make it look good' effect. But looking good is not a long term replacement for actually being good.

You know when you receive a good service at a hotel. In many cases you might be able to quantify why it was good, give the hotel a score for different aspects of the service. You could probably categorise this and formulate a scoring and targets system that any local authority would be proud of. But you don't. You simply continue to use that hotel for future holidays or recommend it to a friend describing its good points. So the human brain is quite capable of understanding and knowing when something is good or bad without the necessity to give it a number or a classification.

And this is the culture that is needed in local authorities. Put staff back into the position where they dedicate their energies to servicing people rather than numbers. The improvements will come – they'll be seen, they'll be obvious – but they just might not be 'measurable'. But those involved will know, whether it is staff, inspectors or residents.

Targets do little more in practice than stifle creativity, discourage entrepreneurialism and ensure that staff and residents are demotivated. By returning to a position whereby qualitative assessments are more important than quantitative targets we will actually start to deliver services based on a desire, willingness and pride in helping local people rather than because we are being dragged along by the promise of more funding.

This approach is a huge risk, of course. It will give more opportunity for staff and managers to hide away and do nothing. But to be honest that's happening now, so why have the huge infrastructure of performance measurement that we have now? It serves no purpose, contributes nothing to front line services, and wastes a huge amount of time and money. But I suspect that while some may hide many more services will thrive and will be in a position whereby resources are freed up and services almost improve by default. But being realistic, even the most inept councils out there would struggle to provide *worse* services with *more* resources.

But the role of inspection is not completely lost in this system. Far from it, in fact – its importance actually grows. But this importance is based around quality rather than quantity. Firstly if inspections are to actually provide any meaningful information then they must be secret. Local authorities don't need to know when they are being inspected so that they have time to prepare the paperwork and organise the ticker tape parade for the inspectors. Think of hotel inspectors: surely the principle of surprise visits and mystery shoppers would work equally well for a number of council services.

For services where this isn't appropriate then the inspections should focus on the service users, the residents who have the dubious privilege of being served by these councils. But again this has to be done properly. Talk to lots of people, investigate things, dig around a little bit. There are always the stooges who love the council no matter what and the moaners who hate them whatever is done. Their opinions need to be tempered by a larger scale investigation into how things are being run.

Council staff should not be ignored in this process but again it should a cross section of staff to make sure that scripts are not prepared and that those officers who might speak out are not hidden away in a convenient broom cupboard for the duration.

Above all the inspections should not be done in a few days sat behind a desk. Far longer is needed and they need to be more frequent. Admittedly this is more expensive but given the savings that are available from cutting all the jobs that do little more than feed information into the targets monster that shouldn't be a problem. However, there is not a requirement to inspect all aspects of everything. To continue the hotel analogy you don't necessarily to visit the hotel laundry to see that the sheets are clean. Some things can be ignored in an inspection, while other things will warrant further investigation. Inspecting from a pre-prepared checklist in a blinkered fashion with no flexibility to ask 'different' questions rarely produces a fair or thorough assessment.

In addition, these inspections need to carry some real power. If they are designed to carry real investigative work rather than simply scratch the surface then their findings are going to be far more reliable. This means that the inspection team can have some real weight. If they find a service or a whole council that isn't up to scratch then they should be able to recommend real actions such as disciplinary action against the weak and the useless; shutting services down; sending in hard-faced and experienced trouble-shooters to run things if the managers can't do it themselves, and so on. Some would argue that inspections can do this now. Well maybe they can but they never do. They send a consultant to advise and assist in service development; they bring with them pretty improvement plans and touchy-feely advice sessions that rarely come to anything.

This approach should scare the living daylights out of those that can't deliver and make everyone else just a little bit nervous. But that's a good thing, because that means change will be coming. It will mean that people will have to be honest which is difficult in the current environment. If a manager knows his service is awful but he wants to work hard to improve it then they should be given the tools to make it better and the support to be able to admit the problems rather than the tools to cover things up. A good quality inspection will help the manager to do this. When working with this type of inspection honesty should most certainly be the best policy and the admission of problems should be applauded as long as the individual and their team are willing and capable of making it better. If they aren't then the exit door can easily be opened for them.

10. The Blind Leading the Blind

"[Local authorities] liked to talk about 'customer focus' and 'service delivery', but actually chose inaction and risk avoidance every time anything but the slightest change was proposed... too often, clients choose to believe that their problems are due to strategy, structure, systems or lack of expertise in their organisation. However, the real problem is actually a lack of management capability or a lack of cohesion in the management team."

– David Craig

Several months before starting work on this book I was sat in a meeting (yes, another one!) along with my boss, three of his equivalents from other services, two senior councillors, the Chief Executive and finally the Deputy Chief Exec. Given the seniority (and salaries) of the people sat around me in the room I had high hopes of the intellect, skills and drive that I would be witnessing. If I'm honest, despite my years in the public sector I am still a little nervous when attending meetings with the top brass, particularly in this instance as it was my first time in these surroundings at my new council.

I needn't have worried. The meeting went without a

hitch, everything was discussed as required and no decisions were actually reached – a typical council meeting in fact. The discussions and interactions were nonetheless a treat to behold, the middle managers pretty much squabbling amongst themselves for two hours whilst the CEO watched on in silence, clearly too bored or indifferent to actually set some direction and get her staff doing something positive. In fairness the inactivity was topped only by the role of the Deputy Chief Exec. What was his role in the meeting? You've guessed it: he was there to take minutes. A man earning £100,000 was therefore sat with a pen in his hand writing notes on those around him. While it is great that a man at this level wants to 'get his hands dirty' doing the menial stuff what's worrying is that this all he did for two hours. Not a word left his lips. I would have hoped that someone in his position and presumably with his skills and abilities might possibly have had more to contribute to a high level discussion than to provide document outlining what everyone said and where they were sat.

Slightly surprised by the Deputy CEO's role I spoke to a colleague who had worked with the man in question on many more occasions than I had. She assured me that this was normal, on the numerous occasions that she had seen him in action he had always been taking minutes, had never made a notable contribution and invariably went to every meeting alongside the CEO where they just sat next to each other watching what went on.

This experience may not sound a big deal but I think it was the straw that broke the camel's back for me and helped make me realise just how poor things really were in local authorities. Those people at the very top of these huge organisations are neither inspirational nor gifted, and even worse seek out mediocrity and avoid decision making wherever possible. Being quite naive I must concede that I expect that those at the very top of local authorities (and every other public sector body) should be inspirational, driven, hard-working, focussed and damn good leaders. In my many years in the field and having worked with literally dozens and dozens (if not hundreds) of managers I can honestly say that I could name perhaps three managers who actually meets these fairly reasonable criteria.

They Just Don't Get It

"Any change is resisted because bureaucrats have a vested interest in the chaos in which they exist."

– Richard M Nixon

The heading of this section could easily double as the title for the whole book. Throughout my several centuries working in local government I have never failed to be astounded by the sheer ineptitude of the general level of management that exists in councils. I try to say this not as an embittered employee or some smart aleck – or at least I am trying not to anyway. I'm trying to express it as someone who is just so disappointed at the way that we manage our public services.

The biggest problem with the management capabilities in councils is the fact that, well, *they just don't get it*. By this I mean that managers don't understand why they are really in post – that they are there to deliver a service – how they fit into everything else that is going on in the council, what the public really want and basically that the majority of what they do is unnecessary, futile and wasteful. I don't know whether it is more worrying that they don't realise this or whether it would be worse if they did realise and chose to do nothing about it. For the purposes of this part of the book though I'll assume ineptitude rather than anything more deliberate or malicious.

When I use the terminology of 'not getting it' I don't necessarily mean that chief executives necessarily need to understand the intricacies of every single person and role in their particular authority. Far from it. In reading various books (well three!) preparing for my first attempt at writing I came across an anecdote from Ha-Joon Chang. He wrote about an event attended by a senior manager from the Kobe Steel Company in Japan, a huge multi-national organisation employing thousands and thousands of people. The manager told an assembled group:

"I have a PhD in metallurgy and have been working in Kobe Steel for nearly three decades, so I know a thing or two about steel making. However, my company is now so large and complex that even I do not understand more than half the things that that are going on within it. As for the other managers, they really haven't much of a clue. Despite this the board routinely approves the majority of projects submitted by our employees, because we believe that our employees work for the good of the company."

The difference between Kobe's managers and the average council manager is the realisation that they don't know everything – that some things lie outside of their knowledge even within their own service and team in some cases. Unfortunately, too many leaders within councils have found a way of knowing nothing and everything at the same time. They make grand claims about taking the strategic view and seeing the big picture when in reality their focus is solely on what is directly in front of them and little else. They are interested solely in their own little empire, their department, and their targets. Working in unison with fellow managers for the greater good is simply not the done thing.

Most managers have little understanding of how their

actions affect the wider community and the big wide world outside the town hall doors. This is not unusual. Who of us truly has a grasp on chaos theory, after all? But the question remains how senior managers in local authorities seem to have so fundamentally lost track of why they are in post.

I have seen dozens of examples of supposedly sensible managers demonstrate immature and destructive behaviour purely in the interest of protecting their bit of the local authority. Again this is something that occurs in the private sector but they aren't playing with your money, they haven't joined their company to make life better for the local community (well not necessarily anyway) and they don't joyfully crow to the public about how wonderfully well they are working together with their colleagues in other services.

Very recently I was meeting with colleagues to discuss a way of developing tourism in the local area. The fact that we have little more than a canal and a roman maze in within our boundaries seemed a little lost on most of those present. The main thrust of the meeting was that to get more people into the area we needed a strategy. This time though there was an added twist. The head of service felt that if we did write a plan, that "We shouldn't include the tourism team on the steering group as they are too operational." I'm not 100% sure what 'too operational' really means and I'm certainly not sure that there needed to be a strategy in the first place but once that was the agreed course of action to not include the tourism team in a tourism plan just because they worked in a different way from how our service manager felt they should seems at best misguided and at worst destructive and infantile.

A week later I was discussing another project with a senior colleague. He asked that I arrange a meeting to discuss a way forward with all the main services involved. A few days later he caught up with me to see how it was going:

Me: I thought it would be useful to invite PT and CG to the meeting, wouldn't it? It's their area after all and they'll be able to advise us on the best thing to do.

He: No chance. They can't come. Not this time. They never invite us to their project meetings so we should manage this one and invite them when we see fit. Just un-invite them.

Something hypocritical in an authority lauded for its ability to deliver great services. But this separation between departments (and most commonly between operational services and 'strategy' or support services) is an all too common theme. Indeed, operational services invariably get the raw end of the deal as they are seen as an unnecessary evil getting in the way of strategy development. In many councils 'operational' has become a dirty word.

It seems that the penny never actually drops with many managers that they are there to serve the public and not to serve themselves and their individual empires. Take one of my earliest manager's briefings at my current council. On a quarterly basis around two hundred managers from across the authority are invited to a half-day session to give out the latest propaganda on how well we are performing as a council and to let us know the most recent policy development relating to diversity awareness.

There is usually about eighty or ninety managers who make it along to these coffee mornings. These are usually the ones with nothing better to do as the more sceptical ones tend to stay away and concentrate on the day job. Meanwhile, those who do attend sit together and are talked at inanely for three hours by the council hierarchy. Rarely is anything learnt or anything positive achieved at these things, but who cares really. It's a nice social occasion after all.

Now and again those present take part in workshops to determine what we all think on a particular issue. At the one session I actually bothered to attend I was sat with a group of about ten other managers and we were asked to discuss the benefits of setting up a central call centre for the authority. The attitude of managers in local authorities was beautifully summed up by just one of my colleagues in response to this request. He simply stated, "A call centre would be a great idea for my team (Adult Services); we waste lots of time dealing with calls from members of the public so at least a call centre would stop us from getting interrupted all the time." The comment was followed by knowing nods around the table and down it went on our flipchart before being presented to the assembled masses.

Something has been lost in the system as intelligent managers have forgotten their reason for being. That public service involves exactly that. Serving the public and making the council as a whole better and stronger. But so many managers have decided it is more important to protect themselves and their empire from all those outside (including making sure they don't any phone calls from bothersome members of the public).

Essentially, the average council manager lacks the character, imagination or bravery to make the difference to the community that they should. Because they see themselves as there to manage what comes through the door to them in a reactionary way they rarely have (or take) the opportunity to stand back and ask themselves whether their service should even be doing it. As a result they feel pressured into just continuing to do more and more of the same thing, resulting in a self-perpetuating cycle of the system getting less and less efficient. This then leads to the managers feeling the need to monitor their staff too an even greater degree and being more defensive to outside agencies or services, feeling that they must adopt a siege mentality rather than one of openness and self-sacrifice.

But then again that might just be me being cynical.

The lack of decision making in councils goes further than just the huge amount of bureaucracy that we have already spoken about. While the strategies, consultations and paperwork all lead to the whole decision-making process being slowed down dramatically the mindset of far too many managers creates another huge problem. The most successful managers are those that attend the most meetings, make the fewest actual decisions, and so are able to hide most successfully. This isn't necessarily about managers never actually leaving their desk (although there are plenty that don't) it is about hiding when the going starts to get tough.

Great Ideas

"Organisation doesn't really accomplish anything. Plans don't accomplish anything, either. Theories of management don't much matter. Endeavours succeed or fail because of the people involved. Only by attracting the best people will you accomplish great deeds."

– Colin Powell

One of the favourite tricks of council management is to adopt 'best practice'. Essentially, this means borrowing an idea from another council, company or country and adopting it yourself to make services better. The idea makes perfect sense; as we are often told why try to reinvent the wheel. All the good ideas have already been had so it is sensible to simply look around for the answer to whatever problem the council might be encountering.

But the world in which councils operate are just too complex to allow this approach to be truly successful. Things are just a little bit more complicated than that. We continue to pick up ideas from other organisations and adopt them into our councils in complete isolation from where the ideas were successful in the first place. Benchmarking, customer surveys, balanced scorecards, business process re-engineering, media relations and social marketing have all been tried and adopted over the last few years in my own authority. All with differing degrees of failure. This failure has been due to the fact that structures, people, systems and the culture are all different in various councils.

To just cut and paste an idea in from elsewhere and then wonder why it doesn't work is simply ludicrous. In reality there are only a handful of best practice principles that any council should look at adopting: strong leadership; openness and honesty; customer care and 'right first time'. Most other best practice becomes a case of copying parts of a flawed system from elsewhere.

I struggled to think of an analogy to use when describing the council management approach but here goes. When you have a wall in your house that desperately needs painting and you have twenty tins of paint in the garage what do you do. You or I might try a few different colours on the wall. Perhaps in a small patch to start with and if it looks like working we do the whole wall. If it turns out that the colour doesn't work on the whole wall we always have the option to let it dry and then paint over it with another colour. This gives the first choice of colour the best possible chance of working and gives us the chance to be flexible about changing it in the future.

A local authority management approach would be subtly different. They would simply throw one bit of a tin at the wall (following a substantial risk assessment). Obviously this won't cover the entire wall so they then grab another tin of a different colour and throw that one at the gaps on the wall. This process is then repeated until all the gaps are filled (or more likely all the tins have gone). The result is a hotchpotch of colours, overlaps, gaps and a general bloody mess that has failed to really address the original need of a wall that needed painting. However, it does have the one advantage that when called to task about the condition of the wall managers are able to say, "Look at all the pretty colours we have used, though."

OK I admit the analogy is a bit laboured but hopefully it makes it helps show just how keen many managers are to adopt the latest management idea. Sadly, the mainstays of good leadership rarely make it onto their list of things to try. If only they were as keen to take some positive action about things or make real decisions. But in the world of the town hall trying a new gimmick is a fantastic alternative to actually doing anything.

I concede at this point that there are things that can be learnt by talking and working with colleagues in other areas. Of course it is worth sharing an approach to something specific that needs addressing. But this should not allow managers to completely replace making decisions or allowing their staff the freedom to get things done.

But in fairness the things that can be learnt from these 'radical' new ideas are perhaps not as much as those in charge would have us believe. At least some of the successes achieved through developing new projects, measurements or approaches can be explained by the Hawthorne effect. Essentially the Hawthorne effect explains that subjects improve or modify their behaviour simply in response to the fact that they are being studied, not in response to any particular experimental manipulation.

In other words once staff are told that they are part of a new approach, a new way of doing things or new measurement, their behaviour changes (often improving results) whether or not the new approach is actually beneficial. It's like a form of placebo whereby the body cures it illness of its own accord simply because it believes it is receiving treatment.

The fundamental point missed by council hierarchy is that the council and the services it delivers are a hugely complex and sometimes chaotic system. And because they simply don't 'get it', managers tend to fixate on one small element of this incredibly complex world in the hope that it will solve the problem. But as we have seen through the targets approach, and the law of unintended consequences, small changes in one area can have unpredicted results in other areas of the system.

But it is important that the baby does not get thrown out with the bathwater. Some of the ideas that do find their way into councils are genuinely insightful and useful ideas that can and should be adopted. But – and it is a big but – these ideas are invariably the most simple and straightforward ones imaginable. They are rarely little more than simple, well thought out (dare I say) common sense judgements. This is not intended as a criticism of these ideas; it is more to point out that simple ideas do not quite justify the heralding that they too often receive. All too often basic common sense is held up and publicised as something akin to genius.

Management by Numbers (Part 2)

"Command and control thinkers expect change to be preceded by cost/benefit analysis, projects, timescales and milestones. Change always starts with a plan. These thinkers think the idea of embarking on change without predetermined outcomes is bizarre. Yet question them and plans are rarely returned to; disasters are buried, milestones are extended, and extenuating circumstances created and are based on opinion rather than knowledge. But people would rather have a plan."

– John Seddon

Some years ago Jamie Oliver started a campaign looking at the low standard of school dinners that were being served to the children of the nation. He went into schools showing us all the now-infamous Turkey Twizzler approach to preparing food. The unhealthy and frankly appalling standard of food being served was a by-product of the management by numbers philosophy that pervades local authorities and which I spoke about earlier in relation to targets.

But the management by numbers approach goes far further than the ridiculous changes that take place in services to ensure that targets are met. In the case of school dinners, rather than their being a target to reach, management saw that the cost of school dinners was the driving force that should overrule any other considerations. When some accountant somewhere worked out that school dinners were costing, say, £1.20 per head, the managers got together and decided that this was too much and a cost-cutting exercise began with the main aim purely and simply of doing things cheaper. No other considerations were made, although positive noises were of course made about maintaining high standards of quality. Gradually and through buying cheaper and cheaper products, the cost will have begun to fall. Below the £1 mark, below the 75p mark, and onwards and downwards. Finally, when the average cost fell to 30p no more money could be squeezed out everyone agreed what a great job had been done.

Sadly, no one actually stood up and said at some point, "Actually everyone, what are we trying to achieve here? How proud should be that we are now spending so little on providing food to the children of the nation?" Surely to continue the trend if we managed to spend less than one penny feeding children we should be ultimately delighted with our achievements. Well sadly, life isn't like that. Numbers mean nothing without context, who decided what the number should be. If we get to 30p is 29p better? No, of course it isn't. If you are in the business of feeding children there are so many other considerations to think about apart from just unit cost.

But unit cost is easy to work out and so is easy to manage. So this is what council managers up and down the land do. Our own authority proudly advertises how much per person it spends on some of its higher profile services. Adverts in the local media proclaim, "Keeping your streets clean for just 88p per day."

What does this mean? Is 88p good or bad? How much should we be spending? If they boasted that they spend nothing cleaning streets would that be acceptable? Of course not, so what number is acceptable? What are we trying to achieve here? The answer is of course a balance between efficiency (cost, if you prefer) and effectiveness (clean streets or good food). This balance is a qualitative one, not necessarily one that can be measured by a pounds and pence figure. Cheap the service may be, but good it might not. As I have said previously, I could undercut any service out there at the drop of a hat, as long as you don't actually want a decent service delivering. After all, the budget airlines are cheaper than British Airways, but does that necessarily mean they are better? If your daughter needed a lifesaving operation only available in the USA for £20,000 would you be happy for the handyman round the corner to do it for £20?

Some managers in a number of councils have twigged onto the fact that sometimes numbers (cheapness) are not the only way of managing services. Many of these individuals have cunningly decided to supplement this approach to making decisions with – yes, you guessed it – other numbers, too. Some managers have rafts of numbers sat before them on their desks. From staff numbers to service user satisfaction, all of these figures are no doubt useful for giving some background information but cannot and will not ever give the magic answers as to how services should be delivered. You cannot type figures into a computer programme and expect it to give you the answer. You need the complexities of a human brain to understand communities, emotions, priorities and all the other things that contribute to this complex world of ours. However cleverly it is put together a formula won't do it all for you.

But gut feel and having an individual opinion is simply not tolerated in local authorities. How would we defend ourselves in court after all if people went off making decisions on things all by themselves? Far easier all round if we let the computer decide what needs to be done. After all numbers are never wrong are they.

But we have already seen with the local government approach to hitting targets that numbers can be used to prove virtually anything and the weaker managers use this to their advantage. And weakness is the word here because managers invariably choose to ignore the facts that are put in front of them; numbers that do not support their view of services are ignored. Again, these traits are true of various members of the human race, but these fundamental problems are deeply engrained into the management culture.

As I started in my current role I was introduced to various members of the management team through a series of meetings. At one of the first ones the main topic of conversation turned to the performance management report we had to prepare for the council hierarchy and the resulting forward plan. Essentially this meant that we had to discuss how we were going to make our department's numbers look as outstanding as possible. We spent the next hour arguing amongst ourselves what the difference was between an outcome, an output, an achievement and a milestone. None of it really mattered of course but it was paramount that we put the right number in the right column; otherwise those in command might type our numbers into the council computer and think less of us.

The meeting changed track a little after this and after we'd decided what an output was we discussed what outputs we should tell other people about. Naturally, it was vital that we were open and transparent but equally we didn't want to look like we weren't performing. The compromise we found was ingenious.

"Let's only show them the good stuff; we don't want to create problems for ourselves."

Of course we all know that these conversations take place but it is quite another thing to witness senior managers actually saying these things. Very simply in that meeting we decided that the numbers were extremely important, and that they would be the basis for all future decision making. In short, the quality of all the public services we delivered would be based on these all important numbers. But ultimately every single one of us in that room were party to a conspiracy to lie and cheat our electorate to convince them they were getting great value for money. When Enron senior management opted for this approach to convince shareholders how successful the business was being they ended up on criminal charges.

But right or wrong, the numbers that management opt for are not used to actually make any *real* decisions. At best they are used to shuffle things (people, funding, paperclips) around. No decisions actually result, people move offices perhaps, managers are shuffled from one team to another but fundamentally nothing changes. No one in control ever stands up to be counted in order to say that this service should no longer be delivered or that we should be moving in this or that direction. The way that decisions are avoided means that the focus is always on the number, the measure, or the target, and so never on what they actually mean.

The Way Forward

Parkinson's Law of Triviality: The time spent on any item of the meeting agenda will be inverse proportion to the sum involved. Thus a £10 million project may be approved in two-and-a-half minutes, while an expenditure of £2,000 – a much easier amount to comprehend – for a much smaller item will be debated for hours then deferred for decision to the next meeting pending the gathering of more information.

Like so many of the things we have seen so far the way forward is easy to talk about but very hard to actually achieve. Management in local government essentially needs to step up to the plate and start being braver. They need to respond to local issues, staff feedback and everything else that comes together to establish what a service really needs to look like. The word entrepreneurial is used a lot when referring to the private sector but the principle needs to be translated into the public sector.

This basically means that managers need to start challenging things. Lots of things, and as much as possible. This means a seismic shift from 'managing minutiae' to actually leading people. Leading people is about creating inspiration, supporting your staff in making things better even when times get tough. This move towards leadership will undoubtedly be difficult and extremely unpopular because as Nixon's quote earlier indicates there are a lot of vested interests. I'm not suggesting wholesale cuts to staff just a huge change in focus about what managers actually see as important.

This shift means that the engrained and backward looking need to be shifted out of town halls. This is frankly no loss. Lots of years of experience disappearing does not have to mean a step backwards. Rather it leaves the way open for those people in local authorities who actually realise that what they've been doing for years is actually unproductive and wasteful. There are plenty of people in councils who are capable of this mindset, but they don't play the game well enough to inch their way up the greasy pole. These are the ones who have been noticed in the past getting things done (admittedly even things wrong in some cases) and as a result have been overlooked as being a bit controversial.

This may sound like I am advocating a move away from measuring everything and that as a result there will be anarchy. This is what proponents of the current system would have you believe – that without management, management, and more management the result would be chaos. This is frankly little more than myth and spin. What is needed is a culture of public service, whereby staff are given one thing to do. Very simply, they serve the public. If it does not contribute towards making the world a better place then it does not get done. No tyrannical management required; no ridiculous performance management tools. Just plain and simple strong leadership, difficult but effective decision making and the guts to make it stick.

But leadership is also about creating a culture where staff are free and able to explore new ideas, to tackle problems head on and most important where they are encouraged to exceed expectations rather than being monitored over every single step they take. Paradoxically the more control that managers try to take the less they actually get. It's like holding onto a wet sponge, the harder you squeeze it, the more water gushes out.

Finally council management needs to start being more honest. Honest about what things are really like right now. Honest about things that don't go well. Honest about who has achieved what.

These shifts in culture will take time, of course, but I'd like to think that it would only take one council, just one, to decide to do things differently. To decide that enough is enough. To start stripping out the deadwood systems and managers. It needs the strongest of chief executives who has the desire to make the biggest of differences, the willingness to be hated and the ability to understand some of the most complex systems and structures known to man.

11. Private Lessons

"Personally, I liked the university. They gave us money and facilities; we didn't have to produce anything! You've never been out of college! You don't know what it's like out there! I've 'worked' in the private sector. They expect results."

– Ray Stantz (Dan Ackroyd), Ghostbusters

For many years councils have been driven to learn lessons from the private sector. We are told on lots of occasions that the private sector is the all singing, all dancing model of how to run an organisation.

This is the point in the book where some of you might be expecting me to wax lyrical about the future of local government resting in the hands of the private sector. Well sorry to disappoint but I feel that the whole private sector approach is a bit of a red herring.

The private sector model has been trialled and adopted in a range of different ways in the councils where I have worked and to date it has failed to make the necessary impacts. Partly because the way it has been implemented has been wrong and partly because the lessons that can actually be learnt from the private sector have largely been ignored and the wrong parts used instead.

I must concede I am pretty ambivalent towards the

private sector itself. From my experience it is neither the panacea that the right suggest it is, nor the unremitting evil that the left would have us believe. Like the rest of the world the private sector is a mixture of good and bad; it has some fantastic people and some real idiots. But as we shall see local government has some very strange approaches to replicating the private sector and working with them.

Quasi-modo!

"Many departments tried to implement a kind of internal market in which they bought and sold services to each other to become more 'commercially oriented' – a process which in general just caused an explosion in the number of administrators and bean counters."

– David Craig

Something that some people may not be aware of is the sheer amount of bureaucracy that exists within councils just in order to quantify how much value for money they are achieving. This is invariably done in order to follow the private sector model of efficiency.

Let me make it clear that it is extremely important that public money is accounted for. I certainly do not advocate a lax approach to showing residents where their hard earned tax money is spent. However, if people really knew how much it costs to actually manage and monitor public money then they may be less critical about a more relaxed approach.

One of the most significant things that councils do to see that they are getting 'best value' out of their various departments is to create what are termed 'quasi-markets'. This rather bizarre name basically describes an attempt by the public sector to create 'open market' conditions in the closed shop of the public sector or in this case the council.

The open market is a wonderful thing out there in the real world of the private sector, without it none of us could expect cheap electrical goods, competitively priced cars or advancing technology. However, in the world of the average council administrator creating an 'open market' becomes an unwieldy mess.

Let me give an example of what these quasi-markets look like. In our council we have a design team, a group of individuals who create a myriad of documents, newsletters and logos. Basically if anyone needs to create a publication for mass distribution then the design team are the people to go to. Now we can have the argument about whether a design team is absolutely necessary in the average town hall (although lots of councils do have one) but let's take a leap of faith and assume that they are a necessity.

The design team like every other department in the council have a variety of costs, mainly in their case for paying staff, buying ink, printers etc. So of course they require a budget to pay for all of this. However, unlike many of the other council departments the budget they receive from the central finance team is not necessarily enough to cover all their costs. So basically this department is left short of funds and must find an alternative source of income.

To get this income the design team basically charge all of the departments who they do work for internally. So if someone needs a leaflet printing in the Highways department they need to use some of their budget (that would otherwise be spent on tarmac) to pay the design team for their time and effort. So basically the money gets transferred from the Highways account code to the Design Team's account code.

This shuffling of money from one internal account to another allows managers in each team to see in detail where the money is going to and coming from like any good financial system. Fundamentally, if printing needs paying for then the money has to come from somewhere so which notional internal budget it comes from is of no real importance at the end of the day. So where is the real harm of this system?

The answer is in the sheer scale in which this approach is implemented. The systems were often originally instigated as a follow up to the now defunct CCT (Compulsory Competitive Tendering) several years ago but the culture remains in place in a huge number of departments. The important thing to realise here is that while the money transferred from team to team in this way is not 'real' in any sense it is purely a paper exercise and the cost to the taxpayer is huge. For every piece of work carried out an invoice must be raised, the invoice must be checked, filed, paid, money transferred, forms filled in. All this takes someone's time. Our small design team of four or five people employ one full time administrator just to manage this paper trail. Remember this person is paid for by your tax money, not to carry out printing or design work, which is the aim of the department (and presumably to save money on potentially more expensive private companies) but just to manage the internal paperwork that does the rounds. This paperwork simply does not need to exist in the real world; it has no tangible benefit whatsoever other than providing council leadership with more figures to look at and discuss.

While the figures for the Design Team might show some fantastic things like a healthy income stream (rather like that of HR discussed earlier in the book) they fail to get to the crux of the problem. Namely that *every* single department in *every* single council I have worked for employs people who have the sole purpose of looking after these internal invoices. Time, effort and resources spent in their millions to show how (in)efficient each department is.

This is just part of the ridiculous approach of adopting private sector principles. Several teams in councils have income targets; not the ones you might expect like Car Parking Teams et al, but rather managers that have been set targets for internal incomes. Again this is not real money it is one department of the council taking money from another department of the council with all the administration that this requires. I kid you not I have had colleagues in the office down the corridor charge me for their time to have a conversation. I expect this if I consult a private solicitor but not from my own colleague in the same organisation.

At one point during this ridiculous charade my manager took me to one side to ensure that I didn't spend too much time talking to my colleague as our departmental budget would only go so far. Really? Paying to talk to each other? Sadly I wasn't able to invoice my manager for the time I spent talking to him.

While many readers in the private sector wish they could charge their own colleagues for their time – particularly if they are wasting it – in practice I feel sure that very few can make it work. For example, if you work in a small office receiving regular external visitors do you want to have to pay an invoice from the receptionist for twenty quid every time they book a visitor in? Does that make the business more efficient in that you can monitor how much work is going through reception? No it doesn't; there are a dozen different and better ways of managing what's going on.

If you still think this is fairly small stuff then think again; whole departments have been created within some councils on the back of this internal market. In my first council we still had responsibility for the area's council housing stock – back in the days before we starting handing housing stock over to other organisations. As you might expect the Housing Team had responsibility for managing all aspects of the housing service. This means that they looked after collecting rents, claiming housing benefits on behalf of tenants (and then subsequently taking the housing benefit back to pay the rent – bizarrely), working closely with tenants associations to get things done, clearing out vacant houses ready for new tenants, carrying out refurbishments to houses, and repairing anything that breaks within the housing stock, from boilers to windows.

The Housing Team understandably had a number of staff to help achieve their aims: Housing Benefit Advisors; Tenancy Support Officers to work with tenant groups; Rent Collection Administrators to arrange collection of weekly and monthly payments, and so the list goes on.

So here I would like to concentrate on the repairs element of the service. How were housing repairs managed? Perhaps the Housing Team had their own tradesmen on the payroll that would carry out repairs and refurbishments as required? Nope. Perhaps they had a contract with a few local builders and they were called in as and when needed? Nope.

The public sector solution was to pay another department of the council to carry out the work. OK, that *might* work! So the Housing Team just called up when a boiler needed replacing, say, and the repairs team sent a man out. The man was being paid from the central pot and so everything was easy. Sadly, no again.

In the case below the managers of the two departments ('Housing' and 'Repairs') reported to the same director and had offices within twenty feet of each other. Anyway this was how the process worked:

1. Tenant calls the housing team to report a broken boiler or whatever – so far so good!

2. Housing team pass the information onto their own repairs manager – er, OK things need checking I suppose.

3. Housing Manager passes the repair request onto her equivalent in the Repairs Team – hmm, fair enough, I guess. The repairs team need to know too although why it is a different team I'm not quite sure.

4. Repairs Team Manager assesses the job and calculates a price to get the job done – OK, a price is needed from someone in the same service because…?

5. Price is sent back to the Housing Manager to agree the price – and so the budget wrangling begins between people in the same office taking their budget from the same place.

6. Opportunity for negotiation on price; period of haggling – makes sense if the money is actually leaving the office but as it doesn't, who is really negotiating with who and over what?

7. Price agreed and Housing Manager arranges for order to be raised by his team on their internal software – can't beat an efficient computer system; good to see.

8. Order sent to Repairs Team – OK a paper trail is important; confirmation needs sending.

9. Repairs Team receive order and raise it on their internal software system – hmm, another system. At least it's keeping someone busy.

10. Repairs Supervisor picks up the order and arranges for the work to be done – hurray, now we're getting somewhere.

11. The appropriate tradesman carries out the work – so let's assume for the sake of brevity that it gets done on time, to a good standard and that no further work is required (although this is quite a stretch from what I've seen).

12. The Repairs Supervisor checks that the work has been carried out and arranges for an invoice to be raised for the work – now we are getting to the important stuff, an invoice, that's what we need more of!

13. Invoice is raised and sent through to Housing Manager – this is where the fun starts as we start invoicing ourselves for work we've done.

14. Invoice is checked off by the Housing Manager – after all we can't trust ourselves to invoice ourselves with the right amount.

15. The Housing Team arrange for payment of the invoice – or in other words 'virtual' money is transferred from one internal budget to another one.

16. Review meeting takes place between Repairs Manager and Housing Manager – a regular meeting to decide whether the Housing team have been ripped off that month. All payments are reviewed and if managers agree then some more 'virtual' money is transferred from one budget to another to make the books balance.

The whole process is repeated thousands of time a year for every repair – and the electorate are suckered into believing that the system is working wonderfully because there's a 'open market' in place and the 'Repairs' team can report a huge 'profit' each year.

This system is one of those all too common ones that occur in councils. One where every single step (even if there are a hundred of them) make sense individually but actually when you look at the whole thing you start to raise an eyebrow and ask yourself why? A system like this has been set up with the best of intentions in mind; to create good value for money. But the Law of Unintended Consequences kicks in and the result is a bureaucratic waste of time that simply creates jobs in administration, estimating and negotiating. All of which adds not one jot to the public value but simply means that paperwork and money is passed from one team of the council across to another. All in the name of a fast and efficient 'private sector' approach, surely any self-respecting business man would not accept this.

Even beyond the overly complex system and ridiculous amount of delays and paperwork this approach created downright animosity between the two managers. The Repairs Manager had a directive to 'make money' – that is, the private sector aim so the powers that be thought it must be a good thing for a council department to operate in the same way. The Housing Department on the other hand are there to provide as effective service as they can on the money they have available. Admittedly there is a compromise to be made between the two individuals in question but in practice life just isn't like that. In reality it created an environment of mistrust, conflict and self-protectionism from two people who should have simply been there to provide a service by working together.

These internal markets basically take everyone's eye off the ball and while managers are busy looking at negotiating prices and making money the actual service received by the tenants becomes of little or no concern to the officers involved. How can this be a better service? Waste everywhere and a service that is adequate at best.

Just compare all this to, say, a production line making baked beans – if the line breaks down the line supervisor decides that an engineer is needed and one is sent for. The engineering team assess the requirements and send someone as soon as possible. All the costs come from the big central pot because everyone is paid effectively from the same budget. Admittedly, you need parts and equipment but these are just another overhead to the company as a whole and are usually a lot less than the 'cost' of the engineers' time to carry out the work. You might argue about the efficacy of individual engineering teams or how costs might be allocated by the finance team, but the principle is largely much easier and more cost effective to manage as a whole.

Is it just me or is the repair system above a little complicated? Why do we make things so hard? Doesn't it involve just a few too many people? Builders and workman are absolutely necessary, as are those dealing with the tenants. But why all the middle men? I'll let you make your own mind up. But if a housing team looks after houses why on earth isn't it more efficient for them to employ a team of tradesman and work hard to ensure that they provide good value for money by keeping them busy. Any additional work just needs a call to a local builder to cover any shortfalls in capacity. After all that's what the Repairs

Team did in this case; and then charged a commission on top for ringing the builder.

The quasi-market invariably throws up some very bizarre ways of working and the most amusing comes from a former boss of mine who is simply the most inspiring person I have ever met during my time in local government. At the time in question we had our own internal warehouse where we stored basic equipment: wood, nails, bin liners, uniforms, etc. Most of the basic equipment that front line operatives would need to carry out their duties. From bin men to grass cutters, window fitters to electricians, most of the materials that were needed could be obtained from these central stores. Sadly, these stores were run as business – no not that we sold to the general public, but rather that the manager of the stores was tasked with making money out of all the other departments who used the equipment. So every bin liner needed a team of administrators to buy it wholesale, mark it up, store it, cost it out to the department who wanted to purchase it, and invoice the appropriate department for it and chase payment for it. Anyway you get the idea by now.

On one occasion my boss Simon needed a sweeping brush to do some work with his team. Down he trudged to the stores with his order form and budget code. He spent his required ten minutes completing the paperwork at the stores and was finally handed his sweeping brush, the head in one hand and the separate handle in the other.

"Can I have a full one, please," he innocently asked.

"No mate, you need to get the joiner to put it together, we just give people these."

Fortunately the joiner was only in the yard next door and Simon called in to ask whether he could take the two minutes required to put the two parts together in order for it to function as intended. Sadly the joiner was also part of the quasi-market and insisted that Simon come back with an order form and budget code; only then could the task be undertaken and the appropriate charge levied. Simon had grown a little weary with the process but bit his tongue and went back to his office to do as he was told just to see how long it would take.

Three days, two order forms, two invoices, four signatures and at least five people and an estimated £100 later the fully assembled sweeping brush was ready and available for collection from the joiner's workshop. Fortunately the broken glass that Simon wanted to be swept up had been removed by the £2.99 brush that he had bought with his own money from B&Q ten minutes after leaving the joiner's workshop on the first day.

Many councils are now changing this approach – not by getting rid of systems or people, but just by altering the paperwork slightly or calling it something different. The upshot being that the hangover of inefficient quasi-markets remains in every council up and down the country and there remains a huge cottage industry that arranges the transfer of the same 'virtual' ten pound note from one department to another on a daily basis.

The Private Way

"What matters to people is not choice but getting their problem solved. To cite examples of choice in various services is to disguise the fact that they are in such a parlous state."

– John Seddon

For some people the best way of solving the culture problem that exists is to send the private sector charging into the town halls on their white horses to pull people up by their bootstraps and to show them how to really run an organisation.

This has always struck me as a rather too simplistic model and doesn't quite reflect the reality of things. The reasoning of the argument being that if a private sector company can run a construction business or a financial organisation then they should have a free go at running the relevant services in the local council. After all, it must have the right people, the right systems, and the right attitude in order for it to have succeeded in the cutthroat world of open competition.

But to simply 'send in the troops' offers little genuine improvement, in my experience. The problem is that when the private sector does come in no matter how well the contract or agreement is set up the companies are still operating in a public sector world. Only by changing these public sector systems completely will the private and public sector be operating on a level playing field.

Competition is great in the private sector as it means we can get a DVD player for under £20 and we can change gas supplier as and when we want. But what is the equivalent for social services? Does an abusive family get to choose which social workers team takes their children from them? Does a street cleaning contract mean that company one will do outside some houses in a street while company two does the rest? This would be the only way that genuine private sector principles are in place.

In reality we end up adopting a pseudo-private sector approach instead. This somehow manages to get the worst bit of both worlds. All the bureaucracy of the public sector combined with the profiteering of the private sector.

As you might be able tell I have something of a chip on my shoulder about the private sector discussion, not because it isn't capable of running public sector contracts but rather because of the various commentators who simply have the blanket opinion that 'the private sector would do it better'. The view that private sector must be 'better' because companies exist in a competitive environment where only the best succeed.

This is a worrying generalisation given what I expect is most people's practical experience of the private sector. Many companies excel at customer service, value for money – or whatever their niche is. However, hundreds of companies cannot claim this; the engineer who came to sort out my boiler a few months was late, expensive, didn't sort out the problem, and was generally a waste of space. Is this the private sector model that guarantees success, according to some experts? Are the CEOs of certain international banking organisations the role models that we should be following? No, of course not.

I have been involved in a number of outsourcing operations whereby a service traditionally delivered by the council has been handed over to the private sector through an extensive procurement exercise – yes one of those! To say they are painful is something of an understatement but once we eventually get through the process of selecting the right company for the job that is when the hard work really starts.

Firstly, it is worth pointing out that some private companies delivering public services works fantastically well. Sadly, these are the exception rather than the rule. The way I see it is that introducing another party into the provision of services simply adds complexity. The council are still ultimately responsible for the service but effectively lose control so that when issues (real or imagined) are raised by the public they are not able to address them directly. Instead they have to be dealt with through a third party and time and money is added in to the system. Either the council shouldn't be in the loop or the private sector company shouldn't be. Take your pick. But if there is a contract in place then someone needs to manage it.

This arrangement for service delivery means that council employees can also take advantage. I have seen managers who would normally avoid dealing with problems at any cost rub their hands at being given the opportunity of managing a private contract. It gives them the chance to wield power and complain about the smallest of things. Companies who simply aim to please are forced to deal with petty complaints just because the contract manager sees it as their duty to make them work for the contract over and above what is reasonable. In short, setting up a private partnership does not magically make everyone involved a better person or a better manager, and hence the service does not miraculously become better. I have seen a number of really good private companies absolutely screwed to the wall simply because they are not in a position to fight back. Either because they are very reliant on council contracts and don't want to rock the boat or simply because they are a company who don't operate like that and want to maintain good working relationships. There is a worrying number of council managers who simply love the extra power and enjoy flexing their muscles.

The actual reason for getting a private sector company in for any given service also worries me. If it is because there is genuine specialism out there and the service actually improves then all well and good. An employment agency tendering to provide staff of course makes absolute sense; similarly a healthcare company tendering to provide occupational health services again rings true. However many contracts have less obvious reasoning and smack of the attitude that 'we can't be bothered to try and improve things ourselves so let's pass the responsibility elsewhere.' It's not our problem then. Worryingly, this approach is becoming the norm as managers start to think it's easier to manage a contract rather than a team of people and a full service.

The method of setting up contracts with the private sector also rules out many companies from even applying.

Any company that wants to help run public services must have so many policies and procedures in place and have so much working capital and make so many guarantees that only larger organisations really stand a chance of being selected. This rules out some of the smaller local companies that know their area well, know their business even better and could actually be capable of providing a great service. Sadly private sector partnerships for most councils mean using the big boys only. Not that this means that the service is bad of course; but it does mean that it isn't the level playing field that the open market brigade might have everyone believe.

A final problem with these arrangements is the impotence that the council really have. However well written contracts and tenders are written the council is invariably over a barrel. If you've got a good company in place then the contract doesn't really matter because they will do the job well irrespective of the fine print. However, if you've got a company who wants to stretch the point then they will. The council awards three-year, five-year and even fifteen-year contracts just like that. They have no intention of backing out of contracts; suing companies for breeching conditions or even really making sure that the service is delivered effectively. Some companies know this and do the bare minimum. Part of this problem is down to poor contract management of course but more fundamentally the very nature of the relationship means that the council is really unable to anything about a company that wants to take them to the cleaners.

Meanwhile the good companies who deliver good services become the 'willing horse' who gets flogged time and time again until it is no longer viable for them to deliver services and the council is forced to look elsewhere.

Monopoly

"Many public services can only be provided by a monopoly. It would make no sense to give claimants a choice over who determines their housing benefits, or to ask citizens who should deal with their planning application. Duplicating services like waste collection to create choice only adds to costs. There are many services for which choice would be economic nonsense."

– John Seddon

One of the main reasons cited for introducing the private sector into the delivery of public services is to introduce choice and competition. By doing this, the theory goes that standards will automatically improve just as it does in the real world of private markets.

The theory is sound, I'm sure, but I have yet to see this competition actually happen. None of the residents in the areas I have worked have ever, ever been truly given choice over their services. The reason for this is that to set up a competitive market in the public sector is just so damn hard. As councils we play at it by creating these ridiculous quasi-markets and by setting up 'partnerships' with the private sector to deliver one service or another. But that isn't about choice it's about delivering basically exactly the same service but in a slightly different and usually more complicated and bureaucratic way.

Personalisation is a recent way of working that has made its way round local government as vulnerable adults (and others) are given more choice over the care support that they receive. The reality of this approach like all the pseudo-private approaches that are used in councils is that they simply add more and more mass to the system. In many cases there simply isn't a market there for the private sector to leap into and manage better. Most of the commercial opportunities that are out there have already been snaffled up by the companies on the ball enough to get in there quickly.

Personalisation just brings about more hidden cost for service users. If twenty private companies want to enter a market to provide, say, adult day care, then they all need checking, monitoring and administering. That's extra cost to the taxpayer. Not only that but the complexity for service users can become overwhelming – more forms to fill in to claim money to then hand it over to various different organisations to receive the same service that they received originally (but without all the forms). It seems a self-defeating way of doing things and often means that it is the parents, families or service user who is most clued up on the form filling that get the best service. Not the ones who are most in need of it.

Again, there is just a lot of bluster accompanied by reams and reams of guidance, newly appointed officers in every town hall and big budgets. All in the name of giving people choice when all they really want is a decent service. The electorate at this time are being somewhat conned into believing they want choice when in fact decent provision would be far better. Seddon's quote above says it all, really. The key point being that all this choice and the extra paperwork that accompanies it adds mass to an already overweight system.

But given the ways that we have seen councils adopt the private sector approach there is little surprise that there is an increasing clamour to see things done better. Even in pure and simple business transactions we seem to get the rough end of the deal. I have touched earlier on our lengthy approach to procurement and the questionable results it achieves. But it goes a little further than that.

I have the suspicion (and I am certainly not alone) that for every contract that is awarded to a builder, a road laying company or whatever the price we pay is fifty percent and even a hundred percent higher than we should be paying. I have no proof other than looking at invoices and balking at the prices and by having a reasonable idea about the cost of things. Take my good friend Bryan, who works in our council's technical team. Bryan is a qualified engineer and surveyor. He works on the team who helps to design and implement new capital schemes, from community centres to road layouts. He works in a team who operate as a quasi-market, so if I speak to him in a formal capacity then it is 'on the clock' so it costs money. Well not real money, but you understand.

On one occasion he was required to carry out a survey on a playing field. You can imagine the sort of thing: finding levels, getting information on manholes and other services. Now Bryan was very well qualified and was very capable of carrying out this work himself. However, because his service was not employed to carry out such work and had a contract with a private firm (Surveys R Us) to do this type of work Bryan was duty bound to pass this project onto them. Several weeks later the survey had been carried out and the invoice arrived. The work had taken one day by the Surveys R Us technician and a further day by their administration. The invoice amounted to £2,000; on top of that the client (in this case the council's parks department) also had to pay for Bryan's time and the appropriate commission. The result was a £2,500 bill to administer and pay for with £2,000 leaving the public coffers and £500 being recycled in the familiar way.

Bryan was astounded at the total cost of this small job but was tied into handing the work out to contract because of the crazy rules that our council insist on implementing to demonstrate openness and competitiveness. Now Bryan and I are friends but I have never found out how much he actually earns. However, given that this job cost us £2,500 I would suggest that even if Bryan had done all the work himself (which he was more than capable of doing rather than just ordering it as he had to) the bill would have been somewhat smaller and the only money paid would have been in his wages. Basically, because the council has access to the skills, the equipment and the resources to carry out the work unless Bryan is on £100,000 a year it must be cheaper and easier for him to carry out the work instead of just overseeing it. The capacity exists to do this if the bureaucracy is taken away. By freeing up the skills of the people most councils already have then the argument of drafting in the private sector en masse becomes utter nonsense.

The Way Forward

"In the civil service we cannot measure our success by the size of our profits; rather we measure success by the size of our staff and our budgets. By definition a big department is more successful than a small one."

– *Yes Minister*

So the notion of getting the private sector in is for me a misnomer. There are as many badly run private companies as public sector ones (well OK maybe not quite as many!). What we have to take from the private sector though are the cross cutting ideas like efficiency, effectiveness, customer service and simple good staff management.

Currently councils have a nasty habit of picking 'ideas' from the private sector and adopting them into structures that are completely different and cultures that do not allow the improvements to be delivered. We then wonder why these ideas do not bring the wonderful improvements that have been promised by consultants or whoever. This is the equivalent of putting lipstick on a bulldog and wondering why the result doesn't look like a supermodel.

There is no doubt that the private sector has a role in helping the council to deliver better services. However, this does not mean handing things over wholesale to the lowest bidder. It means where there is some specialism in the private sector that can be utilised then it should be used. Where improvements need making to services then managers need to bite the bullet and sort them by changing something. Taking the easy way out of giving the problem to someone else should not be an option. This does not solve the problem; it just hides it slightly better.

The way forward then is simple to describe but very hard to implement. Councils need to knuckle down and stop avoiding the problem. The private sector approach solves some problems, but nowhere near as many as some people think. If there are problems with a service then they need resolving. Handing things over to the private sector almost never results in the improvements that are dreamed of so it is vital that problems are sorted at source.

For me the whole idea of introducing private sector choice into services is a strange one. Trying to commission out so many services seems even more ridiculous in lots of cases. The 'contracts' in question still need to be monitored (additional cost to the system); the private company still need to make a profit (additional cost) and the same quality standards still need to be met. In many cases though these standards are not hit and there is little or nothing done as a consequence. So why is it really better to go out to the private sector? The things that need changing are to remove the constraints, the ridiculous requirements and the huge overheads that councils operate with.

12. Miscellaneous, Other, Various and General

In this book so far I have concentrated on just a few of the more wasteful and poorly managed areas of local government. This section aims to bring together just a few more that perhaps don't warrant a full chapter but nonetheless still justify exploring and discussing just a little further.

RISK!

The health and safety culture operating in Britain today is becoming more and more of an issue for those with an ounce of practical sense. Something that is not discussed so extensively is just how much of this 'health and safety gone mad' is actually down to the interpretation by local councils. Nor is it really appreciated just how much time and effort is actually spent by town hall officers in the name of reducing risk and keeping us all safe.

In (slight) defence of the councils here when you understand the financial pressure on managing risk then the picture becomes a little clearer. Councils are responsible for so many services, venues and buildings that the cost of insuring all the activities carried out is massive. I was involved in working with our risk manager at one of my first authorities and at that time (about ten years ago) the insurance bill on an annual basis was more than one and a half million pounds. The authority was neither big nor particularly prone to taking huge risks in the way that services were provided but still it spent this much money (about 1% of its annual budget) on insurance premiums. Extending this principle to all 400-plus authorities it's not unreasonable to suggest that the annual bill to insure councils may be in excess of a billion pounds. Risk management then is *big* business.

As we have seen through some of the cottage industries that have grown up the opportunity to make all that is possible of 'risk management' has just become too good a chance to miss. Don't get me wrong, keeping people healthy and safe is incredibly important but the way that councils operate mean that the emphasis is not on making the world a safer and better place but rather on box ticking, paperwork and being seen to have done something.

The most apparent problem when councils deliver any programme to make their services safer is the sheer lack of common sense that is shown. I know the term 'common sense' is often overused (especially in this book) but I use it here simply to mean that even with all the brain power in the world along with all the available information, sometimes just a smidgeon of real world application (common sense) makes all the difference.

Take the case in one of my authorities of pollarding all the trees along one of the major roads through the town. Pollarding in this case is the major pruning of the branches of a tree, leaving little more than the trunk. This work was done – it was stated in public arenas – to help the health of the trees and ensure they grew better in the future. Rumours abounded in the local press that the trees had been the victims of the health and safety culture that there had been a fear that the branches would suddenly decide to become unattached from the tree and hurl themselves onto the head of an innocent passerby. Sadly, the press rumour was untrue, but the truth was almost as ridiculous. The reason for the destruction of a beautiful avenue of trees and the additional cost of paying a team of workers to carry out the completely unnecessary two weeks' work was very simply a cry of 'a safety issue' from a busybody member of the public.

Our head of service at the time was a real high flier, go get 'em type (very unusual in councils). However, his approach was one that meant decisions were based on what would get him promoted rather than what was best for the town. He'd basically received nothing more than a complaint from a member of the public who lived on the street in question. She had seen children in the street throwing sticks up at the trees to get the conkers down; some sticks had landed in her garden so she had immediately called the council to complain. She eventually spoke to our head of service and played the Health and Safety trump card. If this incident happened again and she was in the garden with her children she would be suing the council for negligence in not dealing with unacceptably dangerous situation. You and I might have been tempted to tell the lady where to stick the conkers in question. Sadly, however, the magic words of 'health and safety' had been uttered. These words set into motion an unstoppable chain of events that no amount of sensible discussion would ever be able to stop. It is because of these magic words, which are used for evil so often, that scores of defenceless trees in a small Midlands town have been mercilessly mutilated at the cost of several thousand pounds. Still, at least everyone is much safer.

So this is only one relatively minor – and on the scale of things inexpensive – example. But in reality it just typifies the approach taken by many council managers. Councils must be seen to do everything possible to reduce risks (however absolutely ridiculous these perceived risks actually are). It is simply not possible to just have a rational debate on whether the risk really exists or whether the risk is such that it warrants the time and expense to deal with it.

Books and websites across the country are filled with examples of this risk-averse attitude and I hesitate from filling another one. Every reader will have seen some ludicrous examples; some apocryphal, others sadly true. But the problem with these risk-averse council managers, policies, and attitudes goes far beyond the obvious impact on services. There is also an impact on wider society. This attitude means that basically every single service is less efficient than it could and should be. Basically, the obsession means that services once again focus on the wrong things.

Take the example of our neighbour who teaches at one of the village schools down the road from us. Last year she was at one of the staff meetings when the head teacher highlighted to everyone there that the lollipop lady who worked directly outside the school would unfortunately be unable to attend work for the following week due to an operation. Unfortunately the local authority had no one else that might be available to cover this absence which meant that there would be no one helping children across the road for that time.

The head teacher (I am told) at this stage was quite concerned about what would happen. She had obviously given the issue some thought though and as a result had come up with a simple four-point plan.

• Inform all children in assembly of what was happening and that they would not be able to cross the road in front of the school for health and safety reasons.

- Send a letter and reply slip home with every child informing parents of the situation and that they must find their own way of getting their children across the road.

- Ask administration team to chase up reply slips from parents and ring round anyone who had not returned them.

- Provide staff near the crossing point to ensure that no children were able to cross the road by themselves (although staff were told that they should under no circumstances help the child in question across the road themselves).

The total cost of printing, staff time and wasted effort is hard to quantify. But suffice to say that our neighbour highlighted that this maybe, just possibly, wasn't the best use of anyone's time. Instead she suggested that she would be more than happy to don the bright yellow jacket and sign and would come to school half an hour earlier each day to see children across the road and stay back a bit later to see them all home.

The ensuing conversation went something like this and demonstrated the ridiculous nature of risk management in local authorities.

Head: I'm sorry Laura; we simply wouldn't be allowed to do that. The advisors in the authority have told me that you haven't had the necessary safeguarding checks to work with children in this environment.

Laura: What do you mean? I teach these children all day every day. I've gone through all the safeguarding checks that are required.

Head: But you need separate checks to work with children in the street to working with them in school.

Laura: Why? They'll be in my classroom two minutes after they've crossed the road. How can I be a risk to children in the street but not in a classroom? I don't want paying extra, you know.

Head: I'm not suggesting you do Laura. It's just not possible. On top of the safeguarding checks you haven't had the necessary training to supervise children crossing the road.

Laura: What? Is this for real? I cross that road with a full class once a week to take them to the sports field at the end of the village. Why am I not allowed to help them across the road one at a time?

Head: Sorry Laura, thank you for your offer but we can't do it. We'll just have to rely on parents to get their children across the road and keep everyone informed of what's happening.

Again, anyone reading the book will be screaming that this is just a case of poor management from the head. But the point here is that the culture in which Mrs Head is operating simply does not allow her any other course of action. She would have had *no* support had there been an accident of some kind. She would have been left high and dry. Indeed, if this worst case scenario had not occurred but snoopers from the local authority had become aware of any alternative arrangements then she is the one who would have been made to feel like a criminal. So the only option open to her is the ridiculously long winded one.

I suppose one might have some sympathy with the head's position but this is the thing about the health and safety culture. Nobody seems to be responsible for the situation. H&S professionals tell us that it's not their fault that overzealous managers misinterpret things; the managers tell us that they are acting on advice; and front line staff are so afraid of making a decision which might have health and safety implications that no decisions are ever made.

One may suggest that the litigation culture in this country is to blame. And to a certain extent the culture of the wider community does bring its own problems as every available opportunity is taken to sue councils. But this is where councils do not do enough to actually help themselves.

Take the inspection of streets and pavements in the towns and villages of the country as an example. Local authorities that have responsibility for the highways usually employ a team of officers who inspect the conditions of all the pavements in their particular area. Their role sounds reasonable enough. After all, the condition of our pavements is important, people should be going round to ensure that our paths and roads are in good condition and repairs are sorted out quickly and efficiently.

In practice things are a little more complicated. In reality the work carried out by these inspectors is driven by the desire to avoid being sued. Pure and simple, any repair carried out to your roads and pavements is driven not by a desire to get the streets looking good or to make sure they are functional and appropriate, but by a drive to avoid going to court. While some may believe this to be sensible enough – after all court cases can be very expensive if someone falls in a pothole – the very fact that all staff are indoctrinated with the avoidance of being sued means that standards, attitudes and cultures are all skewed towards this aim. It's the target culture all over again; the ambition isn't to create well-maintained and safe environments but instead to make sure that if a gap in the pavement goes above the maximum permitted it is 'made safe' as soon as possible. Little or no consideration is ever given to whether the work *really* needs doing, whether the whole road is being ripped up next week anyway, whether there is a pothole that also needs filling in two inches away (but hasn't yet hit the required number of millimetres in depth but might as well be done at the same time). The whole multi-million pound operation is fundamentally flawed because of the fear of litigation and this has once again led to standards slipping, ridiculous decisions being made and ultimately the condition of your roads being 'safe' according to the standards but a big mess by anyone else's standard. The lack of ambition is astonishing really; the drive to do the minimum required means that no one involved in the system can or will ever go the extra mile. Yet still we continue to see men in day-glow jackets out on the streets with their rulers, measuring the depths of potholes, oblivious to the real condition of the wider neighbourhood in which they are stood.

The fear of litigation pervades so many aspects of council life that very few frontline services feel safe. But given the support that these sometimes services receive from their colleagues in the legal and H&S teams there is little wonder. I have been involved in numerous cases, and my colleagues tell me of many more, where members of the public have chanced their arm putting in a legal claim for damages following an 'accident' and have been paid handsomely from the council pot simply because it is too much hassle to fight the case. While at times I can appreciate the cost-benefit approach to things that says if it is going to cost £10,000 to fight the case but only £3,000 to pay off the dodgy claimant then it makes sense to take the less expensive option. But somehow this cheapens the whole process for me; while undoubtedly there are genuine claims out there very few councils have done anything remotely negligent to *cause* accidents. The dodgy claims simply *must* be fought; this is about sending a message (although I dislike the terminology) to false claimants, to say that we won't just roll over every time we are told to.

In one case I am aware of a nameless council in the Midlands received a letter from a No Win, No Fee solicitor informing the Head of Parks that they were seeking damages on behalf of one of their clients whose daughter had lost part of her little finger in a defective gate in one of the city's parks. This was a serious case and obviously prompted further investigation; cue lots of people getting involved without any real impact. The park's manager in question, however, seemed very clued up about how to handle things and started his own informal investigation through his own contacts. It turned out that the small girl in question had actually lost her finger a year before the claim came in, and no record of a complaint of any kind had been received by the mother at that time or any time until the solicitor's letter appeared. Indeed, on speaking to neighbours it became clear that the girl had actually lost her finger in an accident that had happened at home. Clearly the mother had received a knock on the door from her friendly neighbourhood claims solicitor asking if she'd had an accident and decided to give her story a go to see what would happen.

The information unearthed by the manager was taken to the council legal team and he suggested that with further information such as a medical records from the girl's admittance at casualty when it first happened, records of the maintenance carried out on said gate and a myriad of other witness statements that this was most certainly a case that should be fought and that the council could be confident of winning. Sadly the powers that be decided that for 'minimal cost' this case could be paid off, negative publicity could be avoided and basically everyone would forget about it and move on. The family were awarded several thousand pounds in damages, a new gate inspection system was put in place to ensure that every gate in the borough received a monthly visit from staff, and a whole new administration process was created.

My friends in the countryside team have an even harder job to contend with. They are responsible for ensuring that miles upon miles of countryside footpaths are free of holes that people can hurl themselves down in order to claim that they have broken their ankle due to council negligence. It's difficult enough keeping the paths of town and village free of holes without mud and grass tracks having to be inspected and repaired. But still the claims keep coming in and still councils cave in with unnerving regularity.

The health and safety bug seems to be contagious, though. It is no longer the last refuge of statutory bodies. Members of the public now get in on the act too. Any time there is an accident of any kind, or a crime or some other incident reported in the national or local press out jump the special interest groups and community organisations that are there to apply pressure. They demand some kind of action to make sure that this outrage does not happen again. We are *all* responsible for this knee-jerk reaction to life. It has become a sad case of the tail wagging the dog. We as a society have almost gained almost too much control. Every time something does happen and we demand steps be taken councils are too scared not to do something, although of course that something is invariably putting in more bureaucracy and checks. So rather than having councils who are distant and Draconian we actually contrive to make the council overly responsive in some ways.

Take a phone-in programme I heard on a national radio programme a few months ago. The debate was about a school in a small rural village that had a group of parents pressurising the local authority to install eight foot fencing round the whole perimeter of the school. The council had said that the £20,000 budget simply wasn't available to carry out the work. The parents were utterly outraged that the council were unwilling to spend this large amount of money on making their children's school in to a miniature version of Colditz.

What about the paedophiles stalking our streets? How would our children ever be safe from their clammy hands? What about the runaway horses that the village has? How would the children be kept safe from these savage beasts roaming the countryside? What about the joy riders doing doughnuts on the school field? How long before someone is killed in a hit and run incident?

Seriously, these were the comments that were made. There was no evidence that any of these things could or would ever happen. But in the minds of the paranoid, "You just can't take that risk." Now I don't claim that these idiots were truly representative of the majority of parents who probably felt that actually the existing provision of security at the school was perfectly acceptable and that if this type of budget ever did materialise it might be better spent on books, learning resources or a new playground. However, the quiet, rational parents tend not to get a voice.

But no council managers are actually brave enough to listen to the quiet majority in this case. No one in control will ever accept that life cannot be controlled entirely – accidents will always happen, bad people will always do bad things. Councils and the wider state are not the ones who should always be blamed when things go wrong. But the more councils make knee-jerk reactions the more society does blame them. The more 'action' people demand, the more opportunity exists for compensation to be claimed and blame to be apportioned. Councils seem petrified of being seen to be doing nothing, even if that is exactly what should be being done. Image has become everything and actually solving problems has slipped way, way down the list.

The Spin Cycle

"The Law of Inverse Relevance: The less you intend to do about something the more you have to keep talking about it."

– *Yes Minister*

Given the fact that council officials are public servants are employed to simply do what needs to be done, you might think that they would keep a fairly low profile and concentrate on getting the job done. If only it were so.

Councils now seem to have developed a strange obsession for doing less and less whilst informing the public how much of a great service they are receiving. Naturally this reflects the example set by the paymasters in Whitehall. And while the government has it various highly experienced spin doctors, every local council spends time, effort, and money trying hard to keep up.

In every town in the country barely a day goes by without one council story or another appearing in the local newspaper. Whether it is the latest scheme to promote recycling or the official opening of the new extension to the library, the public are bombarded with information on how great their local council is.

In virtually all of the services I have worked in the chance to get a good news story printed or published somewhere or other is something my managers have seen as the ultimate ambition. Even for those individual managers who do not dream of having their faces in the paper there are people around them (directors, councillors or whoever) who feel the need to promote to a wide audience what is happening in their service. This means that someone somewhere is always applying pressure to even the most camera shy managers to make sure that their department gets their fifteen minutes of fame.

"Publicity can be terrible. But only if you don't have any."

– Jane Russell

All the hype that you see in your council newsletter or the local newspaper is managed by the council 'media machine'. The size of this machine varies between authorities, of course, but the principles are the same. "Tell everyone how great we are and avoid bad press at all costs." Naturally this is the drive for every other organisation out there from Pepsi to McDonald's. However, in looking at the waste in local councils, is writing press releases and chasing media interest something you want to be paying for?

In 2007 the Tax Payers Alliance carried out research into the amount of money that each local authority put into their media relations. The results may come as a surprise to the uninitiated. Their finding was that the average council spends close to £1 million pounds on publicity. Again, few could argue against the importance of some level of publicity for councils (we all need to know when our bins will be collected, when the leisure centres are open and how to contact social services in an emergency) but this level of spend seems little excessive to say the least.

So where does all this money actually go? Well as with most council spending the majority is often paying staff (and/or consultants). In short, this is two, three, four or even more media relations officers sat in the town hall monitoring (at least theoretically) everything that goes out to the press or into the public domain. And that is one of the issues I have with the publicity machines in town halls. The media team in many councils don't actually generate the publicity, that task is down to each individual service. So rather than having a private sector style marketing team that are there to produce adverts, publicity and press coverage, local authority publicity teams are another checkpoint, another duplication, another case of double handling to make sure that the press don't get hold of something that is deemed inappropriate. Some might see them as the publicity police. Personally I also see them as just another example of unnecessary middle men.

The way my last authority operated their publicity system beggared belief in terms of making a relatively straight forward thing into little more than a farce. In an attempt to justify their position within the organisation the PR Team created a series of checks and counter checks to ensure that our council presented a united front at all times. The directive was given that *all* contact with the press was forbidden by any individual working for the council. Any approach by any reporter or journalist was to be handled by saying, "I am unable to comment." Any such approaches were to be reported directly to a member of our highly trained and elite PR Team as soon as possible. At which point they would leap in to action.

Me: Hi there. It's just to let you know that I've just received a call from the local paper. They want to do a story on the Town Centre Refurbishment project. I've told them that I can't talk to them without your approval. But they are keen to do a positive article about how things are progressing. They'd like someone to get back to them as soon as possible for a photo, a bit of background and a few quotes from the council. I'm told that we need to contact you to approve everything. So is it OK if I speak to the journalist?

Them: Yes. Bye.

And that's the point about PR teams. Just because they happen to have the phone number of the local newspaper and radio station they think that they are the oracle for all things press related. Sadly it is just not possible for them to know everything about every service so it is always the respective service manager who can answer questions from the press. The 'checks' that the press team insist on being in place really are this feeble. They don't really care about being involved in press stories at all. They are only there to jump down people's throats when a negative story appears somewhere. At which point they simply ask why the manager in question didn't ask for more support from the press team who could have handled the whole situation so much better.

So apart from the occasional phone call from poor saps like me asking for permission to breathe what do the PR Teams do. Well they also:

Manage all press releases – when I say manage what they actually do is *see* all press releases and pass them onto the papers. That's their job – to act as carrier pigeons for the press releases that service managers write. Actually, that's not entirely fair. On some of the occasions that I've been forced to write a press release by a friendly councillor the press team have had some input. After writing the story and sending it onto them they have sometimes returned it with recommended changes. Sadly these changes often involve changing the facts and figures in the story to what *their* records show; altering the meaning of the story and finally inserting a few grammatical or spelling errors. Fortunately they then send it back to the manager for them to correct things before it is made public.

Ensure that councillors *always* get a say – no press release or story that appears in the local paper is complete without a sound-bite from a grinning councillor. That's not an observation, that's another unwritten rule. Whichever party is in power gets 'first dibs'. In other words, if the Tories are in control of the council then invariably only they are given the chance by council officers to comment on the story and to include their own quote. Where you see comments from councillors belonging to opposition parties in the press this is usually because the journalist has been hard-working and chased a comment from an alternative source (rather than simply just printing out the press release as it is received, which happens 90% of the time). Alternatively, it might be because it is approaching election time and the press team feel that they might be being watched by the Ombudsman and so had better be seen to be scrupulously fair.

Count press stories – honestly, you haven't misread that bit. One of my local authorities (in trying to join in with the targets culture) decided that the best way to measure how well the council were performing was to count the number of stories that appeared in the local paper each week. All stories perceived as 'good' were counted and points were taken away for any stories perceived as 'bad'. This meant that each week the communications team sent an email to all staff, giving a weekly total saying, "We've had a great week, twenty-three points so far." The team in question must have had real fun cutting stories out the newspaper for their scrap books for the time that this charade lasted.

Monitor Twitter and Facebook – in entering the latest technological revolution to make information available to people on a rolling twenty-four hour basis many councils have decided that councils should have a social media presence. Many councils have individuals who have responsibility for updating Facebook and Twitter on a regular basis. Perhaps this is wasteful but hardly a big thing. These people often have a larger responsibility to monitor wider web traffic, though. Many local newspaper websites have open forums that allow members of the public to comment on the topics of the day. This often means that they are negative about their local council and it is then that the 'watchers' can jump in by reporting negative or inflammatory to web hosts. Many websites have rules where if three people report a comment it is removed. What is easier than for someone sat at the town hall to make three reports and get the more negative comments removed? I realise this last comment makes me sound just slightly deranged and a bit like a conspiracy theorist but I assure you it does happen in at least two of the authorities I have worked at. It seems highly unlikely that these are the only two councils in the country that have made a start on trying to control free speech in their local area.

All in all the whole management of spin within councils is a little amateurish. Stories in the press are largely ignored by the electorate who tend to have already made up their mind about how well their authority is performing. Local stories very rarely carry more weight than national headlines or having years of experience of receiving services so it makes me wonder who the media teams are trying to kid.

The expanse of local authorities into the area of media stories and mass Twitter releases has been justified by many councils as being more open and transparent. This is a frankly comical justification. Drafting carefully worded press releases is not being open. Councillors blogging on a daily basis with their own political hype is not being transparent. Essentially, writing carefully selected sound bites is not the same as being open and honest about everything that goes on in the town hall. But this is the bizarre thing. When councils (or councillors) are criticised for making decisions behind closed doors they respond with tweets and press stories, believing that they have sorted the problem. But we all know that this just isn't the case. The same problems still exist of dodgy dealing, poor management and all the rest. The stories, tweets and web pages just get better and better at justifying an unacceptable situation.

Awards and Rewards

"Awards are merely the badges of mediocrity."
– Charles Ives

The extent of the publicity and hype surrounding local authorities is not limited to getting a variety of ugly mugs in the local newspaper or churning out good news stories in the council magazines and leaflets. After seeing the Oscars and The Golden Globes on the telly local councils feel that it is only fair that they get in on the awards game. After all they work incredibly hard and it's only right that they get some kind of regional or ideally national award. It's even better if there is a bit of good press to be made. Remember of course that your local council is not a business; it is not trying to get a bit of free advertising to boost its product sales. It is a public body paid for by you to deliver your local services. Why would it need so much publicity?

When it comes to trying to win awards your local council is pretty shameless. As far as many authorities are concerned any award is a good award. No matter who gives them out, what they are for or even if it is actually deserves the recognition that any particular award brings the eyes of politicians and some senior managers light up when that call comes or the letter drops on their desk. So what are these awards actually for?

To be honest just about every service you can think of your council delivering might qualify them to receive a national or regional award. In order to receive the gong, plate or trophy most awarding bodies ask for nominations of some kind. Fantastic you might think; so residents or service users get to put forward their own nominations to national bodies to tell them how great they think their own local council is or how well they have been served by a particularly hard working officer. As ever, though, it tends to work a little differently to that.

The majority (in fact virtually all) of national awards given to councils come as a result of self-nomination. In other words the councils themselves get to complete their own nomination forms telling the judging panel how fabulous they have been performing over the preceding twelve months. Whichever council writes themselves the most glowing reference and attaches the best photographs gets the award. It really is that simple.

Perhaps the notion of local voters having a say in what council gets what awards would just be a step too far for the awarding bodies in question. However, going a stage further, I really must question the relevance and need for these pretty Perspex ornaments. Being the miserable old git that I am I can't quite see the point of things like the Oscars and the Brits but at least the money to pay for these events is not coming from the public purse. The difference with local government awards is that the taxpayer gets to pay for everything. Whether they want to or not.

So what do the public actually get for their money from these awards? Do they come with huge financial gains, sponsorship money, tangible benefits to local public services? Sadly not. However, they do nearly always come with a swanky ceremony in some plush hotel. And as we all know a ceremony must be attended by the senior people who run the service in line for an award. This usually means a councillor, a head of service and a lucky manager or two (naturally very rarely some poor sod actually working on the front line). So the 'in' crowd get to be at the awards dinner, stay over for a couple of nights in a nice hotel, clock the mileage in a hired car and if they are really cheeky even a sherbet or two on expenses. While some of the costs of the ceremonies are picked up by the awarding bodies (which is still usually tax money anyway remember!) most costs get to be picked up by those of us lucky enough to pay council tax.

I shouldn't sound too pious at this point to be honest. I've been to plenty (well a couple) of these awards nights. This is more by pure good luck rather than because I have attained the dizzying heights of senior management for whom these ceremonies are part of the standard perks. I guess this makes me no better than the rest of the public sector in taking advantage of the freebies. The ceremonies are a treat to behold, though; there are literally hundreds of people all being paid by council tax money from up and down the land. Virtually everyone in attendance is pretending that their council is the best, that the tax payer is getting outstanding value for money and that really, "Don't us hard working council officers deserve the occasional treat that these events provide?" And I've joined in these pointless conversations, nodding sagely when some corn-fed councillor starts banging on about how great some service or another really is.

These events represent just more evidence of waste within your council. I have no issue with the notion of recognising good performance in some cases. Whether this is a well done from someone in authority, a letter from the PM or even the occasional MBE chucked out to people. But this ongoing obsession with recognising every single project, service and local amenity in some way or another goes too far.

As with so much that we have seen so far the problem starts to come with the scale of things – with the sheer number of awards that are out there for local councils and their services. Alongside the actual awards there are a myriad of accreditation schemes and charter marks that aim to recognise certain councils' services who have the time to apply.

Back into list mode for a short time I'm afraid but after another half hour search I managed to find nearly fifty national awards and accreditations that your council might want to nominate themselves for. I'm sure if I was a more committed technophile I'd find a hundred more but here's just some of them to whet your appetite:

- Responsible Drinks Retailing Award – a series of awards given to local authorities for their work in reducing drink related issues in their patch.

- Loo of the Year – fairly self-explanatory.

- Academy for Sustainable Communities Award – I have *no* idea.

- CIPFA (Public Servants) Awards – a celebration of the best accountants working in town halls.

- Customer Service Excellence – accreditation and award scheme highlighting the wonderful work carried out by various councils providing 'efficient, effective, excellent, equitable and empowering services'.

- Cemetery of the Year – a necessary service but really do we need awards for them?

- Considerate Constructors Award – well to recognize constructing things in a considerate way (using mufflers on the jackhammers presumably).

- Municipal Journal Awards – dozens of categories celebrating what's best in local government – surprisingly the list is very long!

- Child Poverty Awards – I assume this is to give awards to councils who have tried to reduce child poverty (rather than increasing it) perhaps by handing out cash at local schools; I'm not really sure.

- Local Innovation Awards – 'Celebrates partnerships that demonstrate innovative services, ideas and ways of doing things that bring real benefits to citizens.' Apart from the partnerships charade presumably this is what councils should be doing anyway.

- Council Worker of the Year – I've never been nominated and must say well done to previous winners but really…

- National Transport Awards – 'Rewarding innovation and progress for transport initiatives which are really working.' Er… OK then.

- Stonewall Workplace Equality Index – 'The index celebrates the top 100 employers in the country for fairness on lesbian, gay and bisexual issues.' I'm sure councils up and down the land have plans in place to get their way onto the list.

The list seems endless: Dignity in Care, Member Development Charter; Better Buildings Partnership, Green 500, Wow! Awards, Eco Schools, APSE Awards. But just for good measure councils like to share the love and sponsor their very own award schemes too. In short, they give out awards to their own local residents and companies to get a bit more good press. How about the following:

- Smoke Free Awards – recognizing companies who have 'gone the extra mile' enforcing the smoking ban.

- Your Choice Sandwich Award – pick your favourite sandwich and the council will give who ever makes it an award! (A long overdue recognition I'm sure you'll agree).

- Star Awards – nominate your favourite council employee for a nice gold badge and slap up dinner at the Toby Carvery.

- Local Heart Awards – nominate your local hero for a lovely laminated certificate (cost of award, 12p; cost of administration, £12,000; look on the electorates faces when they find out the real costs, priceless).

It doesn't stop at being given actual awards though; at every public sector seminar and event (and trust me there are hundreds of them) council officers from one authority or another are invited at your expense to present to the assembled crowds. This is usually something less than useful like just how they managed to achieve massive changes for commissioning pencil sharpening services in Lower Whitbury and how this has saved nearly 78p in real terms over the fiscal year.

Whatever your council is actually doing out on the frontline it is more than likely that somewhere in the depths of the town hall numerous officers will be working away furiously on the paperwork for one of the schemes listed above (or one of the many, many more not included). Perhaps there is value in some of them; sharing good ideas, recognizing good work and sharing standard ways of working can be helpful in places. But is it all in the best interest of the residents they serve. Is all the officer time really worth the investment?

I very much doubt it in fairness because it is in all this time and effort that the waste really lays. Of course all the hotels, venues and meals cost money but this money is just part of the overall picture that various Freedom of Information requests paint from time to time. In reality the costs of all these events, awards and accreditation schemes is far higher. Officers spend their time and resources writing award nominations, assessing nominations that come into them, arranging events, writing presentations and then of course attending the ceremonies. Oh and of course writing press releases about the whole saga.

The Way Forward

Having a more level-headed approach to managing risk is linked closely to my earlier comments about management. Having an appropriate response to the dangers is about knowing what to ignore and being brave enough to actually sometimes do nothing. But doing nothing through a conscious choice rather than just sitting on your backside. Councils need to be braver in so much of what they do.

In short, councils need to have the guts to fight more and more of the claims that come their way and learn to say no to far more scare-mongers that inhabit the town halls. The going will be tough at first which is why all the leaders need to be brave; the usual suspects will want heads to roll the first time money is spent unsuccessfully defending a claim but in the long run this approach will start to save money, respect and reputations.

So what about all the money spent on hype and marketing then? Of course I have touched on it already and it doesn't take a rocket scientist to actually work it out. How complicated would it really be to reduce the amount of time and energy spent on promotion. The question has to be asked about how much value for money all this promotion really achieves. While there is undoubtedly information that needs conveying to council tax payers there is absolutely no justification for the huge priority that this area receives in town halls.

Ultimately this means reducing the number of people in the communications and public relations teams. They are simply not needed to deal with the issues that the average council looks after. Service managers across the country already pretty much do their own press releases. Why do we also need the middle men in this case? The messages that need passing out to the local electorate are not and should not be political; they do not need proofreading, checking, and re-drafting. They are there to let people know about forthcoming events or regeneration projects, not to win votes for the ruling party. This way forward then is only an extension of some of my earlier comments about depoliticising local government. It is the political shenanigans that hijack the dealings that councils have with the press. Only when the shabby politics is removed will officers and (independent) councillors be in a position to stop the pathetic games that are played.

At the most fundamental level (and ignoring politics completely) councils simply do not need to 'advertise' the majority of their services. Like the police, the local hospital and a dozen other services council have no need to promote themselves so cynically. The notion of keeping residents informed of the services in the local area is easily done with the minimum of fuss. Politicians and officers hide behind the weak argument that publicity is about consultation and involvement simply to justify spending more money on actually providing less *real* service. Publicity merely serves to spread the word about how well you are being served by the present incumbents. It is this which needs to stop.

Along with these reductions in the size of the media

machine councils need to front up about the awards and accreditations they continuously chase. Recognising the good work of staff is commendable; giving prizes for doing the day job is *not*. So let's move away from the events and seminars and dinners. Let's just concentrate on the day job: manage staff and services well and recognize excellence rather than mediocrity from the best story tellers. Residents deserve better returns on their investment.

13. Paper Cuts

Jim Hacker: *How can we explain saving £32 million just like that? They'll expect it everywhere.*

Sir Humphrey: *Well, just say we've changed our accounting systems or we've redrawn the regional boundaries.*

— *Yes Minister*

As I write the text for this book the political environment in Britain is continuing to go through some massive changes. The coalition government brought with it an unprecedented period of austerity and public sector cuts. As part of this, local authorities have been forced to find some significant savings. Whatever your political persuasion and whether or not you agree with the level of these cuts the fact is that town halls are now faced with the harsh reality of making some hefty cuts.

In looking for the silver lining in this rather scary cloud for town halls the optimists amongst you may be thinking, 'At last, the waste and bureaucracy in town halls will be a thing of the past.' If you have made it this far in the book and still think that then perhaps I haven't got my point across very well!

It will hopefully come as no surprise what my thoughts are on how these cuts are being managed, and on how the new Tory governments changes will be implemented. Call me cynical and perhaps I am being too negative but this is my own take on how these cuts are being implemented.

Early messages

The initial conversations on town hall cuts started around a year before the 2010 general election was even held. At that stage in proceedings senior managers in local authorities up and down the country were having 'serious' discussions about what would happen should the Conservatives be elected. Talk even at that stage was of 25% cuts so there was plenty of notice for all involved.

At the early stages of these discussions I had joined a new team in the local authority and was just meeting some of my new colleagues on the 'senior management team'. The discussions on how the cuts might be implemented were started by our chief executive who had asked all his corporate management team to try and find potential areas for savings in each of their respective service departments.

'Fantastic,' you might be thinking, preparing well ahead of the game, getting ready for potential cuts. Unfortunately not, for twelve or eighteen months I was part of discussions in our own service area that delayed making decisions, talked endlessly about nothing in particular and ultimately decided that we were very lean and efficient anyway so perhaps the cuts should come from elsewhere in the authority.

Actually, I am being a little unfair to the combined intellectual might of our top management. For example at some of our service meeting my colleagues and I discussed the specifics of where savings might be found. It is important to realise that we were at this stage being asked to find 25% savings. 90% of our budget was spent on staff and the people in the room were eight senior managers earning at the very least £30,000 each and most on more. You would expect then some seriously big ideas to come forward and that the managers would be grasping the nettle by both horns and milking it for all it was worth. From memory these were the ideas that were suggested to take forward:

- "Could we make savings on our postage, we send quite a lot of things in the post perhaps we could send more things electronically."
- "Perhaps we should reduce the number of off-site meetings we have, that would save lots on mileage claims."
- "Our printing costs seem quite high; could we print off fewer documents?"

Honestly, I kid you not these were the best ideas we came up with. Essentially the ideas above are sensible for making sure an organisation is efficient; don't use the post if things can go electronically, don't travel when you don't need to etc. But these are not ground-breaking ways to make massive savings and with so much time, expertise and collective salaries sat round the table I think the tax-paying public have every right to expect something slightly more ambitious.

In fairness to my colleagues it is not surprising that this is the best we could do as we were told we could only make savings that did not mean losing staff. On a budget that spends 90% on staff how could we possibly make 25% savings without impacting on staff? Basically, all the suggestions meant was that we would have the same number of staff but they would be operating with their hands tied and have less flexibility to do their work.

Most of the other services and departments across our

authority, in fact all of them came up with the same conclusions. That while there was some opportunity for minor savings, basically we were such a lean and efficient organisation that any significant cuts couldn't be implemented on such a skeletal staff and that no one was prepared to throw themselves on their sword. (Incidentally we have a mere 10,000 staff employed – so we are quite an obese skeleton.)

In short, this left our chief executive in something of an awkward position. Yes, that's right, fear of all fears – she was going to have to make a decision. Well maybe that's taking things a bit far. What she actually did was find some new ways to prevaricate and delegate her decision-making responsibility. Basically after a year of chatting, finger pointing and avoidance we had wasted twelve months of opportunity to get things right and were faced with a new government who literally overnight confirmed our worst fears.

Everything's going to be fine!

"...during these difficult times we [the management] will be making every effort possible to ensure that the impact on staff of these cuts is as small as possible... we will do all we can to safeguard jobs within the authority."

Once the new coalition government were in power I'd like to say that the full might of our collective management ability rolled into action. Instead, while the government and the public were demanding cuts to bureaucracy and public sector waste, our chief executive and elected leaders sent out the above missive to all staff.

While it is hard to be critical of the intention behind this message (to reassure staff and have a positive take on potential cuts) the fundamentals underlying this make it clear that senior management when faced with severe cuts think of staff protection first and public service second. No one is suggesting that staff should not be looked after but in the harsh reality of huge cuts to send out the message that staff will be protected at all costs is frankly irresponsible. No one in the world likes to get rid of staff – the social consequences of laying off a large number of people is potentially disastrous – but when faced with a harsh reality hiding collective heads in the sand creates even more problems in the long run.

In the case of our local authority the head of finance was tasked with finding some initial savings from the collective pot. The initially envisaged 25% savings would equate to about £50 million pounds for an authority of our size so a big chunk of money had to be found (particularly if we were only reducing our purchase of stamps!) Fortunately, within a few weeks of the general election the Head of Finance was able to announce that he had identified £4 million of savings that could be made without having any impact whatsoever on staff or service budgets.

Even the least cynical staff in our department cocked an eyebrow when this announcement was made through the weekly update. Had our head of finance really been sat on a slush fund of £4 million pounds just in case cuts were coming? Where on earth had this £4 million been sat for the last year, two years, or however long? Why hadn't this money been highlighted in any previous efficiency drives (Gerschon etc.)?

To give credit to the man in question I suppose one might argue that for your financial director to be able to identify such a large amount of money with such ruthless efficiency is actually reassuring. That's what financial management is all about, having these pots lying round to be accessed in an emergency, to have contingency plans for when things go 'wrong'. Frankly I see it differently, this is public money. This is tax money paid by every single one of us and to have it sat waiting somewhere in a pot ready to be put up as a saving when needed means that it is not being spent on cleaning the streets, keeping old people cared for and young people educated. If this money had been left for some other contingency why use it for this? What happens if said contingency arises in the future? Or is that not our problem anymore? Everyone should have a problem with this approach to public service management.

And so we are now in the position where the cuts are being delivered. There is simply no ignoring that fact now. However, the nature of the cuts is still open for local management to decide and therein lays the problem as the rest of the book shows.

Those people ultimately deciding on where the cuts will come are not the average person in the street, or even the people really delivering the front line service. No. It is a selected number of the elected members and senior management. In fairness in any organisation that needs to make cuts in the public or private sector these are the people who make the decisions. However, in your average town hall this is like giving the lunatics the keys to the asylum.

As the cuts are implemented in each local authority there are a number of keys problems that town halls struggle to overcome. The signs are now there that the cuts do not mean more efficient local councils for Joe Public.

Management approach to efficiency

As part of the council's drive to make efficiencies, even before cuts were being talked about, every member of staff (at least those on email!) received an edict from senior management. It basically stated that the cost of processing each individual invoice that came through the council was in the region of £50. After picking myself up off the floor and cleaning my spluttered tea from the computer keyboard I read the rest of the email. It essentially said that due to this 'high cost' we should all be making a conscious effort to reduce the number of invoices that we produce. In short, any invoices under £x were no longer going to be processed and due to the efforts of all staff it was hoped that we would many have less invoices to process as orders should be combined where possible.

To me the message sent out above has a few common sense issues to raise, No doubt the high power managers and accountancy boffins can put me right on this one though.

My initial question on this is how the £50 per invoice figure was reached. My assumption is that this is not an actual price to actually process an actual invoice. As a council we don't work like this, our processing team work through the pile of invoices they have, and despite the advent of quasi-markets, don't (yet) charge other services £50 per invoice to get it through the system. Instead they pay their staff from the centrally allocated budget, and then work through everything that needs doing. This is essentially a sensible way to work. Even if the target and measure focused managers out there don't like it.

Instead I would suggest (in fact a little bird told me) that management took the number of staff in our various finance teams, added up all their wages/time spent processing invoices and the associated costs and then divided that figure by the number of invoices we get in a year. So if it costs us, let's say, £1 million per year to pay all the staff to process 20,000 invoices you get to your £50 figure. However, if the drive is to just reduce the number of invoices then surely this alone does not mean it becomes cheaper to process invoices. It just means we are processing fewer invoices and so the average cost per invoice actually goes up. In short, instead of simply focussing on the number of invoices, which admittedly may need to be examined (why process twenty invoices from one supplier when one will do), we also need to be looking at the overall system of how invoices are processed. Why are there so many people involved? Why does it cost '£1 million' to process the invoices in the first place? Can we lose people from the system if we are doing less processing? These all need to be answered as well if savings are to be actually made.

What is the point in reducing the number of invoices we process if the overall cost of processing the invoices remains the same. In other words, if we process half as many invoices we need half as many people to do it (or even less if we can actually make the system more efficient into the bargain). This doesn't mean redundancies necessarily it just means moving people onto other tasks if they are there. But the message from management is not, "Let's be better," it is instead, "Let's massage the numbers."

However, local authorities don't work like this; reducing costs by reducing staff is not an option. What we need is headline figures to impress the local politicians with. What we do is find a figure that sounds like it means something (£50 per invoice) and then try and manage it in isolation from the system from which it was plucked. In other words, trying to make changes based on a number at the bottom of a page rather than by rooting out what the number means, understanding its real context, and making hard decisions based on what that number and lots of other pieces of evidence really tells you.

This is problem number one with the way cuts are being managed in your town hall. Numbers can be and are used to demonstrate just how hard hitting the changes are, despite the fact that numbers as we know can show just about anything that those in control want them to. But the attitude of management is resolute. If the numbers show a saving then there *must* be a saving; even if common sense dictates otherwise.

I would suggest that savings are only savings if we are spending less now than we were before. However, as the next section demonstrates this isn't always necessarily the case.

When is a saving not a saving?

"The government actuary department identified a saving of £117,000, achieved by moving their stuff and rented a floor in the Human Tissue Authority. Hence one government department is paying another and this counts as an efficiency saving. It also counts as a profit because the new subtenant is buying the department's services.

"Savings do not require that efficiencies be recorded net of up-front investment costs i.e. if you spend money to save money, you count the money saved but not the money spent in the process. By this logic, scrapping posts and hiring in consultants counts as a total saving."

– Matthew Elliot and Lee Rotherham

In these times of reduced spending most people in Britain, except those who are fortunate enough to have won *X-Factor* or be a Premiership footballer, may well have looked at 'tightening the belt'. We all understand what we mean by that term in the real world: it means spending a bit less than we were this time last year. Maybe we will go out for fewer meals each month. Maybe we'll put off buying that expensive new suit or pair of shoes. Maybe it's Bognor rather than Barbados for the family holiday (sorry Bognor!).

These are all sensible if unappealing ways to spend less. And it's certainly less problematic than selling one of the kids, although that is certainly tempting at times. However, for the average local authority, making savings means something completely different. Rather than being a practical and at most times tough decision-making process, based on real examples where one thing has to be given a higher priority than something else (paying the mortgage rather than the golf club membership) town hall managers have a get out of jail free card when faced with cuts. They are called 'efficiencies'.

What are efficiencies in this context? I hesitate from passing on the various full descriptions that I have been given as frankly now you've got this far in the book I'd be disappointed if you now hurled it with extreme velocity in to the far corner of the room.

Instead I'll give you an abridged version. Efficiencies are effectively savings that come in two kinds: those you don't necessarily have to be able to 'bank', and those that you do. The second being what you and I might actually recognize as a 'cut' i.e. spending less actual money.

The first type are what councils prefer to go for and are those things that rather than being a real cash figure are activities that your department might be doing more efficiently. For example if you find a way of doing a task 10% quicker than before you get to claim for 10% savings. That means if the bins are collected thirty minutes quicker the service can claim this as a saving, even if the bin lads don't actually use that half an hour to do anything else productive. (While efficiencies can be monetary savings they are only 'counted' if it doesn't have an impact on services. So sacking all the bin men doesn't count as you won't be collecting bins any more. Fair point, really.)

Now don't get me wrong, I'm all for making services more efficient but surely, shouldn't savings be just a little more tangible, and perhaps at some stage involve real money and real savings? We are told by central government that efficiencies should include a mix of cashable and non-cashable savings, but if you were in the place of a local authority manager which one would you be looking at primarily – theoretical paper savings or hard to manage real savings?

Efficiencies are an accountant's dream. Some wonderful paper savings can be made without actually having to go through the tricky process of really spending less. So now that the hammer has fallen on local government budgets all the accountants have been well and truly prepared. Not just with their various collected slush funds that they have kept up their sleeves for just such occasions but also with a series of paper savings to impress whoever comes in to check. For me this is changing *nothing* in local government, it merely changes what column the accountants add up their different beans in.

We have already seen in other parts of the book that services (i.e. those bits that tax payers actually seem to want to see) are the lowest of the low in town halls. This situation sadly does not change when it comes to determining cuts. Once the creative accounting systems, slush funds and other jiggery-pokery have been used up, councils may have to find some actual cuts.

As these cuts are implemented unfortunately it is highly unlikely that they will ever get implemented on a needs or priority basis. They don't result from open and honest discussions amongst all those involved in any changes. Instead, they come from the accountants locked in a room with the chief executives and leaders of each council. Given the poor relationship many direct delivery services have with their corporate centres this can only finish in one way. Changes are being poorly planned and even more poorly managed.

Our authority has talked about that magic 25% figure for cuts over some period of time so finding out that the actual cuts were to be significantly lower than that came as a huge relief for all involved. No council management team or group of councillors would ever admit it but when the level of cuts to each local authority was announced every single person involved were simply delighted. That hasn't stop them grumbling about how unfair the cuts still are, but then what would you expect?

But the planning for these did sadly not involve senior management sitting down and prioritising services, seeing what local people can do without (advisors, bureaucracy, consultants, cottage industries etc.). Instead, they have said, "Right, the 'fairest' way of managing these cuts is to ask each service/department for the same percentage cut each."

On the face of it this seems a sensible approach. When large private organisations need to make cuts it is sometimes an approach they use. However, there is a difference, whether the marketing team or the research and development team different services within a private company are working towards a common purpose, increasing profits. In a council the common purpose it not so clear, public service is a common aim but supporting old people in their homes and writing a strategy on the council's new approach to tourism are not the same.

So the same percentage cut across all services leaves us in a quandary; each council is structured very differently, but who is to say that a council's strategy development unit 'deserves' the same level of cuts as social services. Or neighbourhood services need the same level of cuts as the IT unit. Surely to implement standard cuts across the board is the worst kind of decision-making avoidance by senior management. It is something that makes sense on paper but not in practice. If the local electorate want their priority to be social services and not strategy then perhaps social services should face 0% cuts and strategy development 80% cuts… just maybe. But then again that would require guts and brains.

Cutting budgets not people

I talked in the early part of the chapter about the conversations that our management team had in the early days about where cuts might come from. One of the limitations that was set even then was that we should only be looking at spending that does not reduce staff numbers.

This was a message that was reinforced when our elected leader indicated her intention to safeguard jobs and this sadly will be the ongoing approach to making cuts at councils up and down the country. Just to emphasise that no one wants to see people lose jobs, but equally, if savings have to be made then money spent on employing people has to be in the mix with the rest of any savings.

To give an example, let's look at how money is spent by any council. Effectively, there is money spent on paying people and the rest is spent on the things they need to do their job. So you pay for the guys (and girls) who fill in the potholes on the roads, but you also buy their shovels, spades and tarmac. You pay for social workers' wages but also for their computers and software systems to track people and their mileage claims to go out and visit families.

So far, so simple then? But as every single council is so petrified of letting people go they will ensure that every other avenue is explored first. This means cutting these operational budgets first before staff are even looked at. Imagine it, your local council employs ten guys who fill potholes. By reducing their operational budget they might save ten percent of the overall spend. Sadly, the department can only buy 50% of the tools and tarmac they used to, meaning they can only fill 50% as many potholes. Result! No redundancies and those that are employed get paid the same amount of money to do 50% less work. Another victory for idiocy over common sense and the town hall apparatchiks over the local tax payer.

This might be a slightly facetious example but the principle stands. If you retain the same number of staff as much as possible and simply slash the budget they have to do their jobs with what's the point in employing them. Environmental health officers who can't visit restaurants because the petrol won't be paid for, administrative staff that can't print things out or send mail because they don't have the money, or maintenance staff that can't repair things because they are unable to purchase the spare parts – the list goes on.

The need to increase efficiency is clear, but this principle should already exist. For example, mileage for staff should be reduced as much as possible, but the minute budgets start to disappear for the core functions of any post then the post itself starts to become unworkable. It's like running a hospital with a full complement of doctors, nurses and support staff but without the money for drugs, bandages, and other treatments. It starts to become nonsense. The bottom line looks great but rather than the efficiency increasing in line with the level of cuts you end with services getting exponentially worse. Staff are and will continue to be protected at the expense of service delivery.

An example of this was demonstrated in a local authority area in the North East of England. On a national news feature it was described how this council had made some initial savings following central government's announcements of cuts. They had achieved nearly two and a half million pounds of savings. Where from? Yes, you've got it, not from waste and bureaucracy, but by taking away investment in new play areas for young people, from bus pass provision for pensioners and for mobility schemes for the disabled. And I am confident that as a result of these cuts the public will be more heavily affected than council staff.

The ones to stay will be the ones no one else wants

Once all the above approaches have been exhausted local authorities eventually reach the stage where they need to ship some staff. Without wishing the dole queue on anyone even the kindest amongst you might be thinking, 'About time too.'

However, this is where councils encounter yet another difficulty. Who do they get rid of? There are a couple of ways of losing people. The first one requires people to leave of their own volition. Anyone who leaves the authority during difficult times simply because they get a better offer is a heaven-sent gift for the management team. It doesn't matter who they are, the fact that they've gone without having to be paid redundancy is a great bonus. Our council, and many other others like it, have opted to try and get even more value out of the departure of staff by freezing recruitment and not replacing those that leave.

This sounds great in theory and brings some real savings, but it hardly demonstrates dynamic leadership. When cuts are demanded shouldn't those at the top be looking at reorganising what they have to focus on priorities, ensuring that every member of staff is deployed most effectively, cutting jobs that can be done without and generally moving the pack around to ensure front line services are those that continue and the waste is reduced.

Now call me cynical, but just because certain staff have left that doesn't mean that they're the people that can be done without. Or that they are the ones that would have been shipped out in a sensible and well thought out restructuring of services. More subtly, nor does it mean that they are the ones with the skills that we should be losing either. Indeed, I'll go further. At a time like this the staff that we do actually lose are probably the very ones we should be fighting to keep. The best ones start to desert the sinking ship quite quickly.

But this isn't how senior management and elected members think. What they see is a number at the bottom of a page. If the number says that they must save the equivalent money to 500 staff what could be easier than waiting until 500 people have left the authority. While there is nothing wrong with utilizing 'natural wastage' of staff to manage change, the key word here is 'utilise'. Not just waiting for it to happen and hoping that it takes place in the right areas. Let's be honest, the chances of the right 500 people leaving is a million to one.

Still, this approach is far easier than actually having a deep and thorough understanding of 10,000 people and all the services that they deliver. Far easier to sit back and wait for things to happen. This ostrich approach to management should be something you are now familiar with from this book.

There is a second stage to losing staff. Given that all the necessary savings are still unlikely to be achieved through waiting for people to leave then redundancy will have to be considered.

Let's be honest, redundancy in the private sector has certainly been used in the past to clear out posts and, more importantly, people that no longer have a place in the organisation. So my hope is that the first to go are the dead and the dying of the council, i.e. those who have been there since before the war. Again, when it comes to practice it is not as simple as that. Some people have been with us for so long that to pay them off would bankrupt an average Middle Eastern oil sheikh. This means that redundancy costs have to be built in to any plans to get rid of people. Rather than it being a case of getting shot of those that need to go then it is a case of keeping those that are most expensive to get rid of.

Again, I'm a practical person. That is how life is.

Sometimes finances need to take precedence. However, sometimes, just sometimes, perhaps management should be able to see that on their list of people they should take other things in to consideration as well as the numbers. Perhaps person X is the person who should stay despite the fact that they are cheaper to get rid of. Perhaps they have the vision, the skills, the potential and the ability to really achieve something. Just the sort of person that the average council should be fighting tooth and nail to keep. But no. Despite the huge emphasis that councils place on 'human resources', sadly the numbers game will always win over a good, positive approach to making cuts.

The Way Forward

Whatever the future of local government holds, cuts will eventually hit home in some form. Sadly rather than being the panacea that the government and wider society hopes I fear that the cuts are doing little more than reaffirming and strengthening the current problems that are faced by the average council. Few changes that take place in local authorities actually alter systems and improve ways of working. They simply add to existing processes rather than replacing them. This leads to a huge 'hangover' of twenty or thirty years of ideas, plans, systems and restructures (and people).

So rather than being an opportunity for the deadwood to be removed and bureaucracy streamlined it has become a chance for the empire builders to increase their stranglehold on the system and for the status quo to be maintained – but with poorer levels of real services for the public. Only if the leaders out there choose to overcome the things I have discussed above will the cuts mean a positive future for the average town hall and the residents it serves.

Senior managers need to be a whole lot more public spirited. It is all too easy at this stage to play the politics game and blame others for the situation. This of course solves nothing. Cuts, as they filter through, very simply need to avoid the pitfalls that I have outlined above. Changes need to be made positively to deal with the lazy and the weak. Redundancies need to be used to remove the deadwood. Cuts should be managed by knowledge, understanding and where necessary self-sacrifice through a return to public service over self-interest. Numbers need to be seen as little more than indicators so that the accountants should be told what to do rather than being the ones doing the telling. Savings should mean savings and not simply become a case of shuffling the numbers into different columns.

The best people should be encouraged to stay while the yes men and sycophants should be politely booted out. Those in control know exactly who these people are but have kept them close through self-protection and a desire to build their empires. Like the walls of Jericho it is time that these empires crumbled and things were started over.

Currently stories up and down the country tell of more cuts to well used front line services. Care homes being closed, bus routes being cut and so on. This is the approach that needs avoiding at all costs. This is the nasty political side of the cuts as councillors start to reduce the 'popular' services and get to blame the government. This provides the opportunity for people to say, "This isn't our fault; the nasty government made us do it." This is not true. The cuts are harsh but ultimately the local leaders still get to decide *where* the cuts actually come and this provides the perfect opportunity for local management to finally do the right thing.

"During WWII the Ministry of Labour were going round the country to try and identify anyone working on large country estates

that might be utilised in war work. Keen to do what he could to support the war effort one particular duke agreed to the survey being undertaken on his staff. After much research the ministry man presented his findings to the duke.

"'Well sir, having spoken to everyone we can see the need for you to have a butler, a valet and three footman. We can see the need for a chamber maid, an upstairs maid, a downstairs maid, two charladies, the in between maid and the two ladies maids. We can also see the need for a driver, a handyman, two stable boys, a groom, a head gardener and four under-gardeners. We can also appreciate your need for a head chef, a sous chef and four kitchen staff. But sir, do you absolutely need TWO pastry chefs?'

"The Duke's immediate and simple rebuttal was, 'My God. Can't a man have a biscuit?'"

– As recounted by Stephen Fry on QI

14. Final Thoughts

"How many times can a man turn his head and pretend that he just doesn't see?"

– Bob Dylan

So there you have it, my humble, prejudiced and utterly one-sided view of the wonderful world of local government. I concede that my opinions are not well balanced and that I have ignored many, many cases of things working perfectly well. Perhaps my time working in the midst of all this mismanagement and bureaucracy has addled my brain I'm not really sure. However, one thing I do know for sure and that is things could be far, far, far better than they are at the moment.

Councils are the nearest point of contact that the majority of citizens will ever have with the agencies of government. Admittedly in a majority of cases councils are there simply to enact national priorities and policies but it would only take one council in the country to make that leap into the unknown and start doing things better for a real difference to be made to public services.

If local government entrepreneurs are given their head, and the appropriate support from above, then they could make a genuine difference to society. Not on things like defence policies but on real quality of life stuff. These are the things that people see and interact with on a daily basis and so these are the things that are very important.

And this is where the government and local councils have a difficult balancing act to carry out. We need to concentrate on actually doing fewer things but doing them a damn sight better. As councils we need to take away the bad systems, the targets and the reliance on others holding our hands, the bureaucracy, the politics and the low expectations.

The future can be genuinely bright; councils have the potential to really raise their standards by working with their communities. I genuinely believe that. But in order to really make a difference they need wholesale changes. No more tweaks, no more subtle amendments to policies and strategies. Any changes that are made from now need to use dynamite to dislodge the ensconced attitudes, opinions, people and systems. I just hope that someone out there in power is brave enough, capable enough and determined enough to really make it work.

As a final point I am reminded of one very simple anecdote from a source that I have long since forgotten. It is about a flood that sadly hit a town in the north of England some years ago. As the flood waters rose it trapped a mother and her young baby in the first floor of their house, leaving them with no means of escape, and they faced the very real danger of drowning. Terrified of what to do next, the mother's heart leapt as she saw a small boat floating past the just below the level of her window on top of the torrent of water.

Seeing the trapped pair the two men on the boat manoeuvred their small vessel as close as they dared and shouted over that the mother needed to hand over her baby to them. The mother saw that the men were wearing high visibility vests and undoubtedly worked for the local council. Because of the speed of the water she realised that they would have to double back to come and collect her later and that her baby would be in the hands of strangers for some time. She paused no more than a split second before reaching out over the flood water, risking her own life and that of her baby, to pass the most treasured thing in her life over to two perfect strangers who she may never see again. Her reasoning was simple: they're from the council, of course I can trust them. No risk assessments, no DBS checks, no paperwork. Just trust, community and human spirit.

If a member of the public is able to place such trust in an unknown individual simply because of the name on their vest then the potential for good to be carried out by the organisation that person represents is incredible. Isn't it time we made something more of this potential for doing good?

"Peace will come to earth when people have more to do with each other and governments less."

– Richard Cobden

References

"I love quotations because it is a joy to find thoughts one might have, beautifully expressed with much authority by someone recognized wiser than oneself."

— Marlene Dietrich

Carswell, D & Hannan, D (2008) The Plan: Twelve Months to Renew Britain. Douglas Carswell and Daniel Hannan.

Chalk, F (2006) It's Your Time You're Wasting. Monday Books.

Chandler, JA (2009) Local Government Today. Manchester University Press.

Chang, HJ (2010) 23 Things They Don't Tell You About Capitalism. Allen Lane.

Clark, R (2006) How to Label a Goat. Harriman House.

Collins, J (2001) Good to Great. Random House Business.

Copperfield, PC David (2006) Wasting Police Time. Monday Books.

Craig, D (2005) Rip Off. Original Book Co.

Eliot & Rotherham (2006) Bumper Book of Government Waste. Harriman House.

Gadget, I (2008) Perverting the Course of Justice. Monday Books.

Goldacre, B (2008) Bad Science. Fourth Estate.

Seddon, J (1992) I Want You to Cheat. Triarchy Press.

Seddon, J (2008) Systems Thinking in the Public Sector. Triarchy Press.

Semler, R (2001) Maverick. Random House Business.

13968138R00161

Printed in Poland
by Amazon Fulfillment
Poland Sp. z o.o., Wrocław